ENVIRONMENTAL DECEPTIONS

The Tension between Liberalism and Environmental Policymaking in the United States

Matthew Alan Cahn

State University of New York Press

Published by
State University of New York Press, Albany

For information, address State University of New York
Press, State University Plaza, Albany, N.Y., 12246

Production by E. Moore
Marketing by Theresa A. Swierzowski

Library of Congress Cataloging-in-Publication Data

Cahn, Matthew Alan, 1961–
    Environmental deceptions :   the tension between liberalism and envi-
ronmental policymaking in the United States / Matthew Alan Cahn.
        p.   cm. — (SUNY series in international environmental policy and
theory)
    Includes bibliographical references and index.
    ISBN 0-7914-2263-1 (alk. paper). — ISBN 0-7914-2264-X (pbk. : alk. paper)
    1. Environmental policy—United States.   2. Liberalism—United States.
3. United States—Politics and government—1945–1989.   4. United States—
Politics and government—1989–   I. Title.   II. Series.
GE180.C34   1995
363.7′00973—dc20   94-6017
                                                                                        CIP

10 9 8 7 6 5 4 3

For Diane, Alex, and Marcella,
and for Noa, who spent far too little time with us.

Contents

List of Tables

Acknowledgments

This project has benefitted from the insights and criticisms of many people. Early drafts were argued over with Diane Berger and Aaron Chankin. I am not sure whose view prevailed, but I at least had the last word. Early feedback was also generously provided by Sheldon Kamieniecki, Mark Kann, John Elliott, and Ann Crigler. Mark Kann and Rory O'Brien were instrumental in helping me understand, to the extent I do, the normative implications of liberalism and the environment.

Sheldon Kamieniecki has been particularly instrumental in helping me think through the themes in this book, as teacher, mentor, colleague, friend, and editor. His imprint is stamped not only on this work, but on me as well.

Understanding and support were provided by my colleagues at California State University, Northridge, particularly Gene Price, Jane Bayes, Stella Theoudoulou, Mort Auerbach, and for financial assistance—making early review of several chapters possible—Dean Ralph Vicero. Research assistance was tirelessly provided by Steven Tandberg.

Clay Morgan and the production team at SUNY Press must be acknowledged for their guidance and professionalism.

Finally, I must thank Diane Berger, my partner in all things academic and otherwise, for her constant feedback, patience, and understanding. I must also apologize for falling into a career path as strange as this.

I alone, of course, remain fully responsible for the shortcomings in this text.

1   The Political Economy
of Liberal Public Policy

Introduction

Environmental concerns have become increasingly important over the last two decades. By now most people agree that measures must be taken to improve environmental quality. Environmental improvement, however, poses a difficult challenge to the American policy process. To understand environmental policy in the 1990s one must confront two distinct influences: the legacy of Lockean liberalism in American political culture; and the propensity of policy makers to "market" public policies through symbolic language.

Liberal society is fundamentally limited in its ability to resolve the problem of environmental degradation. There are two structural tensions between liberalism and environmental quality. First, liberalism's emphasis on individual self-interest creates a problematic concept of communal good. Society, as manifest in liberal contract theory, exists not to find some higher good, but to protect individual rights. Communal good is limited to providing a stable environment for individual rights. As a consequence, individual and corporate property rights have consistently overshadowed community claims on resource management. Second, capitalism, as a system of economic production and distribution, has been characterized by a constant drive for expansion in search of increased productivity and profit. The impact of that expansionary ethic has been overuse of limited resources and the degradation of our physical environment.

In the United States the tension between liberalism and environmental quality has been consistently understated in policy debates. Policy elites, seeking to resolve environmental problems while maintaining economic growth, have reduced complex environmental relationships to simple issues, suggesting that modest regulation will effect substantial improvement. In this sense, environmental policy has been largely symbolic. Environmental policies are consciously engineered both to create and to satisfy public demand. The public articulates vague needs, which are then adopted by policy makers who respond with specific goals, cuing public opinion into "attainable" policy options. Public demand is then satisfied with relatively soft regulation.

This study does not argue that every piece of environmental legislation that has fallen short of its stated goals is "symbolic." Rather, in failing to address the inherent tensions between liberalism and environmental quality, policy makers are necessarily understating the complexities of environmental degradation. As such, environmental policies are designed to deal with problems that have been consciously oversimplified. It is in this sense that the policies are symbolic.

The literature on environmental politics is concentrated in two areas. Policy studies tend to focus on descriptive data (e.g., Lester 1989; Vig and Kraft 1994), while normative analyses tend to prescribe an environmental wish list (e.g., Milbrath 1989). This study integrates normative analysis with empirical data in an effort to explain the structural limitations liberal society faces in improving environmental quality.

This book begins the analysis of environmental policy with attention to the parameters of American political culture and the inherent limitations the language of liberalism places on American policy choices. Chapter 1 explores the role the liberal political economy in the United States has played in defining communal need and discusses the implications for environmental policy. Specifically, the chapter examines how liberalism in the American context affects environmental policy choices. Chapter 2 applies the literature on symbolic policy and the engineering of consensus to the analysis, arguing that environmental policy is typified by legislation that appears strong, though in reality remains largely unimplemented.

Ultimately, the study explores the substantive policy areas of concern to the environment in an effort to explain the evolution of specific policies. Chapter 3 defines the environmental policy subsystem, focusing on bureaucratic decision making and the infrastructure of establishing environmental priorities. Chapters 4, 5, 6, and 7 explore the issue areas of air, water, waste, and energy respectively. As these areas account for most public concern and governmental action, they provide useful case studies in examining the tensions between liberalism and environmental quality. Similarly, the chapters explore how symbolic politics have been used to ease these tensions.

The study concludes by suggesting that the challenge presented by environmental degradation may force a rethinking of the traditional liberal self-interest model. If policy choices continue to be constrained by our ideological inheritance, the future is bleak. Yet society is not static, and as environmental resources become increasingly deteriorated and toxic, it is likely that traditional notions of property rights will be re-evaluated in light of an evolving notion of communal good. The concluding chapter will use Hardin's "Tragedy of the Commons" (1968) as a conceptual tool to contrast the narrow Lockean self-interest model with a Rawls (1971) based communitarian model to illustrate the opportunity for Liberal redefinition.

A Note on Evaluative Criteria

Evaluating environmental policy success is a difficult and often ambiguous endeavor. Policy analysts often equate disappointing policy outcomes with policy failure. But such analyses often ignore incremental improvement and behavioral changes that may lead to greater improvement over the life of the policy (Bartlett 1994). For example, while Superfund (CERCLA) has been widely criticized as a failure due to the large amounts of money spent on litigation and the relatively few successfully cleaned sites, the liability clause in the act has forced behavior changes that may significantly reduce future contamination (Dinan and Johnson 1990; Bartlett 1994). Determinations of policy success, then, depend on how evaluative criteria are defined.

Lest this study be grouped with the growing literature predicting environmental apocalypse, I will be explicit in defining the intent of this analysis: this book attempts to explain the implications of evolving American political culture on environmental policy making, and ultimately environmental quality. The analysis concludes that while the existing framework of environmental regulation has provided incremental improvement, the extent of potential environmental improvement is necessarily limited by tensions within the existing political culture.

The evaluative criteria utilized in this study include five elements: the strength of standards and goals using public health and resource management as primary concerns; timetables and deadlines; rates of compliance and enforcement of standards and deadlines; the extent to which lifestyle changes aimed at improving environmental quality are encouraged; and the extent to which alternative technologies aimed at reducing degradation and improving environmental quality are required. Chapter 3 explores these criteria in greater detail.

Lockean Liberalism and Public Policy I:
The Problem of Communal Good

American political culture has evolved from an awkward marriage of two disparate philosophical legacies: civic republicanism and Lockean liberalism. Several observers note that civic republicanism was favored by prerevolutionary thinkers (e.g., Wood 1969; Appleby 1984; Pocock 1975; Kann 1991). Wood (1969) argues that the American revolution was not merely economic, but philosophical, as colonists attempted to replace British autocracy with a federation of autonomous nation-states. Kann suggests that, "the ideal was that virtuous Americans would rise above self-interest, participate together to found state commonwealths, and balance liberty and authority for the public good" (1991:5). Civic republicanism, in this sense, placed public good before individual self-interest.

The Republican potential, however, began to unfold as political and economic elites became less and less convinced that common people—nonelites—were virtuous enough to place public good ahead of individual passions. In this sense, Shays' Rebellion became emblematic of the founders' fears. Daniel Shays, an army captain during the revolutionary war, led a group of farmers—most of whom were war veterans—in a rebellion intended to prevent foreclosures on their farms by keeping the western Massachusetts county courts from sitting until after the next election. In placing their self-interest before the interests of the state—and the financiers who stood to benefit—Shays and his colleagues shattered the Republican model.

Civic virtue, in its classic sense, requires citizens to sublimate their individual passions for a common good. Early American political thinkers came to doubt that destructive individual passions (lust, greed, avarice) could be suppressed. Thus, if it was not possible to create a virtuous society, it was possible to create a society in which self-interest could be harnessed productively. If citizens could not sublimate their self-interest for a common interest, they could channel self-interest into economic productivity. The Liberal self-interest model came to eclipse Republican civic virtue with a social stability based on economic self-interest. But, as Pocock (1975) suggests, while the self-interest model may have replaced the civic Republican model, the discourse on civic virtue remained, albeit in a different context. Appleby (1984) points out that by the end of the eighteenth century the classical meaning of civic virtue—rising above private interests for some public good—was replaced with an alternate, even contrary meaning. Civic virtue became synonymous with individual industriousness and achievement. The result may be understood as a sort of latent civic virtue: economic self-interest as public interest.

This view permeates the Liberal discourse. Schumpeter (1942) saw no public interest apart from individual self-interest. Citizens participate politically to the extent that they have self-interested goals and desires. Similarly, elected policy makers pursue public policy goals to satisfy the demands of the electorate, in the self-interested goal of re-election. Hartz (1955) and Macpherson (1962) argue that "possessive individualism" diverts the passions of men (laziness, self-indulgence) into a drive for economic gain, creating sober, productive citizens. Downs (1957) and other "Public Choice" scholars see self-interest as the primary motivation of all people.

The infusion of this latent civic virtue into Lockean liberalism creates a uniquely American liberalism where public good is defined by incrementally increasing individual good. In this sense American liberalism remains true to its utilitarian roots: the common good is the aggregate sum of individual good. Thus, the role of the community is to provide the infrastructure to make the pursuit and enjoyment of individual rights possible. In Lockean terms, the public good is provided through the creation of a stable environment for the acquisition, use, and disposition of private property. As a consequence, Liberal society is fundamentally organized around economic interaction.

The policy implications are twofold: Liberal policy seeks to create independent economic actors; and Liberal policy demands that any communal need be evaluated in light of individual property rights. The primacy of Liberal individualism creates a dilemma for public policy: Lockean individualism is nowhere manifest more strongly than in its commitment to individual property rights, and as a result, individual property rights limit the notion of communal rights, creating a problematic definition of communal good.

Self-Interest and the Public Good

Civic virtue has been alternately defined as altruism, self-control, sobriety, productivity, and love of country, in short, self-sacrifice in the public interest. As a tempering influence on self-interest, civic virtue succeeds in creating citizens who can live side by side in a stable political environment. The problem from a public policy perspective, however, is that Liberal civic virtue, to the extent that it exists, remains privatized. What is missing is a notion of communal rights. There is no language of public interest apart from individual interest, leaving the scope of public policy choices severely limited.

The self-interest versus civic virtue debate in liberalism inevitably raises questions about altruism and examples of communitarianism. The nurturing of children and the elderly in families, volunteering in church or organizational activities, contributing to charities, alumni support of schools, and participating in the civic operations of neighborhood communities and towns are all widespread in the American experience. Bellah and others (1985), McWilliams (1973), and others present a vivid picture of the various communities in which Americans participate in the search for social support networks. However, such communitarian participation takes place almost exclusively on the subnational level. Family, church, union, school, town, and so forth, all offer identifiable community values with which members can identify; civic participation allows a sense of belonging. In this sense, self-sacrifice for the "good" of the community carries personal implications: improving the "community" directly improves one's immediate environment. As such, public interest and private interest are the same.

Communitarian involvement on the state and national level is much more difficult to identify. The only consistent self-sacrifice we see on the national level is military service. Yet, even military service provides a problematic form of civic virtue in the traditional sense. Historically, most soldiers came to "serve their country" through conscription, a not-so-subtle coercion. Perhaps today's all-volunteer army is a result of civic-mindedness. More likely, however, is the perception that military service provides some sort of personal opportunity. Individual self-interest may be a greater factor than civic virtue. College aid, job training, and veterans' benefits are major inducements. Military public service, then, may be conducive to self-interest. No one was more surprised by the U.S. deployment of five hundred thousand troops in the Persian Gulf than many of the soldiers themselves. Many had enlisted, not to become citizen soldiers, but to gain steady work (Wilkerson 1991).

The Search for a Common Good

Liberalism is based on individual self-interest as the foundation for preserving life. Society, as manifest in the social contract, exists not to find some higher collective good, but simply to ensure individual rights. The proper role of Liberal government, then, is to protect a narrow scope of individual rights (self-preservation, liberty, and property). This definition of public good justifies the creation of an infrastructure which makes such protections possible: a police force and army; public laws which define a consistent system for the accumulation, use, and transfer of property; courts to arbitrate between competing interests; jails to house those who have violated the norms of Liberal society; and ultimately, a structure to measure the aggregate individual good—elections to choose representatives for public office. Beyond this, Liberal government has little authority.

In the absence of an explicit language of communal rights, there is little prospect of limiting concrete property rights for an abstract public good. The narrow Liberal definition of communal good has consistently allowed individual and corporate claims of property rights to outweigh the need for serious environmental regulation, as the following chapters will show. As a consequence of the parameters imposed by the problematic Liberal definition of communal good, the American policy process is fundamentally limited in its ability to confront environmental issues adequately.

The notion of communal good in American liberalism has evolved to accommodate specific problems that threaten the fabric of social stability. Public education programs evolved to encourage social integration (Peters 1993). New Deal liberalism, particularly through programs such as social security, developed as an accommodation to economic disintegration (Bowles and Gintis 1986). Yet, while traditional definitions of communal good remain narrow, environmental degradation may force a new approach. To the extent that environmental destruction is understood to threaten social stability, American liberalism's latent civic virtue may resurface. Rawls' (1971) restatement of justice as a central Liberal priority may provide the bridge.

Rawls accepts self-interest as the primary motivation in human society but rejects the utilitarian influence that has come to characterize Western liberalism. Rawls broadens the self-interest model to accommodate a communitarian ethic in the tradition of Kant. Rawls identifies two basic principles necessary for a just society:

> First: each person is to have an equal right to the most extensive basic liberty compatible with a similar liberty for others.
>
> Second: social and economic inequalities are to be arranged so that they are both (a) reasonably expected to be to everyone's advantage, and (b) attached to positions and offices open to all. (Rawls 1971:60)

In this sense, procedural justice exists when equal people give informed consent to the process by which decisions are made (Wenz 1988). In such cases, the decisions, regardless of outcome, are "fair."

Further, Rawls defines just policies as those that benefit the least advantaged within the society, in addition to anyone else. In this sense, "there is no injustice in the greater benefits earned by a few provided that the situation of persons not so fortunate is thereby improved"

(Rawls 1971:15). This reflects Rawls' notion of *pareto optimality*: "a configuration is efficient whenever it is impossible to change it so as to make some persons (at least one) better off without at the same time making other persons (at least one) worse off" (Rawls 1971:67).

Rawls' concept of fairness and of *pareto optimality* are useful for expanding the traditionally narrow liberal self-interest model. Within the Rawlsian paradigm, self-interest itself must include minimizing social bads, because any one of us may, at some time, be exposed to those bads. Self-interest is maintained, then, when individuals vote to finance greater fire protection services, since any one of us can suffer the tragedy of being in a burning building. By this logic, it is possible to argue that minimizing environmental degradation is a form of maintaining individual self-interest, because any one of us may find ourselves, for example, exposed to toxins that have seeped into aquifers. Wenz (1988) suggests that in establishing a common fund to clean up abandoned waste sites CERCLA (Superfund) is an example of just environmental policy—in the Rawlsian sense. Rawls reintegrates the language of civic virtue into a utilitarian liberal discourse.

The tension between public rights and private rights is nowhere felt more strongly than in environmental policy. Environmental policy is predicated on regulating the use and development of private property. Without redefining traditional Lockean property rights, environmental policy proposes to legislate what property owners can and cannot do with their property. Traditional concepts of Liberal civic virtue say nothing to this dilemma. But, as Rawls suggests, it may be possible to accommodate communal challenges by redefining self-interest. A Rawlsian alternative is discussed in detail in Chapter 8.

Lockean Liberalism and Public Policy II: The Tension between Public and Private Rights

Locke's concern with property was a function of survival, not greed. One's property would ensure self-preservation, and ultimately liberty. The role of the state, therefore, is to protect private property (Locke 1963:2.124). If property rights were ensured, individuals would be able to take care of themselves. Sustenance, liberty, and security are all a function of material wealth. As a result, Liberal policy decisions have traditionally been subservient to economic concerns.

The Lockean emphasis on private property poses a quandary for the American policy process. While politics is considered a public sphere, property remains a private sphere. As a consequence, there is often a conflict between political power (public power) and economic power (private power). While Liberal society encourages collective participation in deciding our political fate, our personal fate remains vulnerable to economic domination. Several observers (e.g., Dahl 1985; Bowles and Gintis 1986) see a growing sphere of authoritarianism within the corporate structure of Liberal capitalism.

At the same time, the public sphere itself remains vulnerable to private interests. Clearly, the pluralist model of counterbalancing elites mediating interests has proven inadequate. The theoretical work done by Mills (1956) and the empirical work done by Dye (1986), Domhoff (1983), and Presthus (1974), among others, suggest that rather than competing, the interests of economic elites tend to cohere in key policy areas. Not only are the number of corporate interest groups and PACs at an all-time high, but the structure of the policy-making establishment has come to replace Democratic agencies with private think tanks (Reynolds and Vogler 1991; Guttman and Willner 1976).

The Brookings Institution, RAND Corporation, Council for Economic Development (CED), Council on Foreign Relations (CFR), and others form the bridge between corporate interests and government. The think tanks are considered by many policy makers to be neutral policy consultants and are thus extended great access to the policy-making arena. Yet virtually all of them have strong foundations in the present business community. The RAND Corporation was created as a joint venture between the U.S. Airforce and the aerospace industry as a think tank devoted to the theory and technology of deterrence. The CED was founded in the early 1940s by a consortium of corporate leaders to influence specific policy formation. The CFR was founded in 1921 by corporate executives and financiers to help shape foreign policy (Domhoff 1983; Guttman and Willner 1976).

Public life has remained subservient to private interests in other ways as well. Public policy, consequently, must place explicit economic concerns above a public interest that remains abstract. Reagan's executive order 12291 simply puts into formal practice long-established beliefs:

> In promulgating new regulations, reviewing existing regulations, and developing legislative proposals concerning regulations, all agencies, to the extent permitted by law, shall adhere to the following requirements: . . . *Regulatory action shall not be undertaken unless the potential benefits to society outweigh the potential costs to society;* . . . Agencies shall set regulatory priorities with the aim of maximizing the aggregate net benefits to society, *taking into ac-*

count the condition of the national economy. (Executive Order 12291, sect. 2, clauses B and C; emphases added)

Such a policy is reminiscent of the narrow benefit-cost calculation that allowed Ford to continue building Pintos with unsafe fuel tanks between 1971 and 1976. The calculation made by the National Highway Transportation Safety Administration (NHTSA) in 1972 showed that deaths and injuries resulting from fuel leakage in otherwise minor accidents would cost Ford $49.5 million annually in damages. Correcting the defective design would have cost Ford—at eleven dollars per car—$137 million annually (Dowie 1977). While cost effectiveness is an important element of policy analysis, the reliance on a narrow benefit-cost calculation to evaluate policy has created perverse policy consequences.

Even eminent domain, which many describe as an example of governmental initiative to secure the public good, is more accurately defined as governmental action on behalf of self-interested policy elites. In *Berman v. Parker* (1954), the Court held that the government had a wide constitutional authority to seize private property for a compelling public purpose (Lowi and Ginsberg 1990). But the history of eminent domain seizures is characterized by the displacing of the poor. In *Berman* the Court cleared the way for the removal of dilapidated housing in the District of Columbia to make room for a new development. While there is a public interest in renewing urban areas, the previous residents were effectively displaced, as the new housing carried substantially higher rents. Freeways and transit systems are routinely built on property seized from working-class people (Piven and Cloward 1982). It is not surprising that eminent domain seizures tend to occur in poorer areas. Residents in wealthier areas have the legal resources necessary to make seizures difficult. As a consequence, eminent domain replaces a general public good with a limited, even affluent, "public good."

The distinction of political rights as public and economic rights as private has created a dynamic that typically places property rights outside the restraints of public policy. As a result, policy makers are limited in their ability to regulate resource management. The following sections explore the evolution of the American market economy and its implication for environmental quality.

Liberalism and Capitalism

The relationship between liberalism and capitalism is not accidental. Rather, Capitalist economics is a function of liberalism. If liberalism is predicated on the pursuit of individual self-interest, much of this pursuit is economic in nature. Friedman (1982) argues that individual freedom—the ability to pursue one's self-interest—is predicated on economic freedom. Adam Smith (1937) argued that a system of self-interested independent economic actors would not only maximize individual freedom, but would maximize social good as well. The economic equilibrium that Smith anticipated would, in fact, create social stability. The necessary components of a Capitalist economy—private property, competitive self-interest, economic liberty, minimal government—are precisely the same components present in a Liberal society. Thus, while liberalism and capitalism are not the same animal, they are mutually dependent upon one another.

Like liberalism, capitalism has evolved over time. Market failures over the past two centuries, most notably the depression in the 1930s, have shown that capitalist economies are not necessarily self-regulating, and great disparities in income distribution have made legitimation of classical economics more difficult. The American political economy has gone through several changes, each in the attempt to maximize economic stability and productivity. Thus, while American capitalism has evolved over the years, the nature of economic interaction reflects the central values of liberalism: the pursuit of social stability through self-interested economic interaction, and the protection of private rights to property.

The Evolving Infrastructure of American Capitalism

The constitutional basis of American political economy provides for Republican government, with only limited citizen participation. The insulated relationship between elected officials and the electorate suggests that the framers intentionally sought to protect the Union from "popular passions." The electoral college and indirect election of the president, the appointment of senators by state legislators until 1913, single member districts which preclude minority party representation, judicial review, and the state-imposed gender and property requirements all ensured elite supervision of popular participation. In establishing a framework for the acquisition and transfer of property, the contract and commerce clauses protect economic interests from Populist intrusion and provide a stable market environment.

Fletcher v. Peck (1810) expanded the contract clause to include the notion of vested rights (that property is the basic social institution and the *raison d' etre* of the state is to protect private property). Later, in the Dartmouth College case (1819), Marshall and his colleagues found that states have no power over corporate charters other than "what is expressly or implicitly reserved by the charter itself" (Justice Joseph Story, in Mason and Stephenson 1987:274).

The commerce clause was included in the Constitution specifically to prevent the states from interfering with free commercial interactions. The interpretation of the clause has followed the Marshall Court precedents. In *Brown v. Maryland* (1827) Marshall wrote:

> It has been observed that the powers remaining with the States (police powers) may be so exercised as to come in conflict with those vested in Congress. When this happens, that which is not supreme must yield to that which is supreme. . . . The taxing power of the states . . . cannot interfere with any regulation of commerce. (In Mason and Stephenson 1987,172)

The Marshall Court decisions reinforce the sentiments that the convention delegates clearly intended the Constitution to embody. Specifically, the Constitution and Court decisions protect commerce from interstate trade barriers and protect the national market economy. Such protections on commercial interaction pose serious problems for government attempts to regulate property or commerce on behalf of some collective good.

By midcentury, the development of the railroads and canal systems, and the introduction of new technologies—including the clipper ship, the steam engine, the reaper, and interchangeable machine parts—created an economic infrastructure that allowed for rapid industrialization and a shift away from the traditional agrarian economy. In this climate, business structures moved from small decentralized proprietorships to large centralized corporate organizations (Markovich and Pynn 1988).

By the 1890s the growing centralization of capital in large corporations threatened traditional interests, such as farmers and merchants. Ultimately, pressure from a vague coalition of farmers, laborers, merchants, and other small business enterprises resulted in limited antitrust regulation. Heilbroner (1977) notes that this governmental intervention was seen as necessary so as to allow the economy to regulate itself more efficiently and thereby grow more equitably.

The consistent economic growth through the 1920s seemed to confirm this belief. Between 1921 and 1927 per capita income almost doubled—growing from $440 to $817; similarly, between 1923 and 1927 the Dow Jones index tripled (Markovich and Pynn 1988). In the end, of course, this did not last. In October 1929, Adam Smith's economic equilibrium exploded. By 1933 GNP fell from $104 billion to $56 billion. It became clear that increased governmental intervention was necessary.

The series of New Deal legislation—including the Emergency Banking Relief Act (1933), the Emergency Farm Mortgage Act (1933), and the National Industrial Recovery Act (1933)—sought to create financial security and market stability. These policies were not intended to move the economy away from capitalism. Rather, they were meant to rescue capitalism. The practical necessity to intervene in the economy during the early 1930s led to the acceptance of Keynesian economic theory.

Keynes argued that economic stability relies upon spending—by consumers, business, and government. Government should stimulate this spending through direct expenditures and a redistribution of income so as to ensure a stable pool of consumers. In this way the Keynesian paradigm created the American welfare state. New Deal programs—such as unemployment insurance, social security, and supplemental security income—sought to stabilize unemployment, and increase consumption, thereby expanding economic production.

By the late 1970s, however, the optimism with Keynesian economics began to fade. Growing inflation, rising unemployment, and the continued presence of poverty created an atmosphere of frustration and intolerance. Within this climate Reagan came to office promising to improve economic growth by reducing governmental regulation, moving policy-setting and financial responsibilities back to the states (New Federalism), and through supply-side economic policy which would encourage business-sector growth rather than consumption (Markovich and Pynn 1988).

While the evolution of American capitalism has allowed for greater governmental intervention, it has not moved beyond the parameters of liberalism. If liberalism equates the common good as the aggregate of individual good, then governmental intervention to improve economic growth is consistent with liberal principles. While American capitalism has changed over the years, these changes reflect the central values of liberalism: maximizing individual self-interest to create a property-based social stability. As a consequence, each stage in the evolution of American capitalism has had similar implications for environmental quality.

The Tension Between Liberalism and Environmental Quality in the United States

Capitalism, as an economic system establishing supply and distribution of goods, is largely inconsistent with the collective good of maintaining environmental quality. Liberalism equates liberty with the ability to acquire, use, and dispose of private property free of government intrusion.

Capitalism encourages environmental degradation in several ways. As the Marshall Court articulated, Liberal society is based upon the rights of private property (economic liberty). As such, the state has limited authority to mandate how citizens use their property. Environmental policy, on the other hand, is predicated on the regulation of private resources and behaviors. If, in the view of liberalism, the chief end of civil society is the preservation and protection of property rights, environmental regulation challenges the ideological basis of political order.

Economic success in capitalism has historically been defined by economic growth. To maximize individual and corporate profit, and to minimize recessionary contractions, capitalism has relied on continual economic expansion. While one would expect the GNP to grow consistent with the growth of population, the drive to maximize profits pushes greater efficiency from available resources and expansion of markets to maximize productivity. As production increases, ever greater materials are required, straining, and often destroying, environmental resources. And, extensive industrial and agricultural production has created vast amounts of waste, including sludge, heavy metals, salts, and toxic chemicals that are released into the air, water, and soil.

While population in the United States grew by 39 percent between 1960 and 1990, GNP rose by 150 percent (see Table 1.1). This greater productivity came as a result of new technologies that made industrial processes more efficient and production materials cheaper. But, this was not without a cost. During the same time, energy consumption increased by 85 percent (Table 1.2) and municipal solid waste generation increased by 91 percent—more than twice the rate of population growth. Moreover, the demand for natural resources jumped, illustrated by a 75 percent increase in timber extraction. And the reliance on toxic chemicals soared, as illustrated by a 60 percent increase in pesticide use (see Table 1.3). Environmental stress is a net result of unbridled economic growth.

Furthermore, as a system of individual economic actors (including corporate actors), capitalism encourages pollution by punishing those who would clean and reduce waste with a reduced profit margin. It is far cheaper and easier to simply dump waste than to reduce, reuse, or reprocess it. Even those manufacturers who wish to be good corporate citizens are slow to employ pollution reduction technologies voluntarily, because to do so unilaterally would put those corporations at a competitive disadvantage. Pollution is an economic externality in that polluters are able to shift the cost of polluting to the society as a whole. While environmental degradation is certainly not unique to capitalist

TABLE 1.1. U.S. Population Growth, GNP Growth, and Municipal Solid
Waste Generated 1935–1990

Year	Population (millions)	GNP (billions of 1982 dollars)	Municipal Solid Waste Generated (million tons)
1935	127.4	580.2	na
1940	132.6	772.9	na
1945	140.5	1,354.8	na
1950	152.3	1,203.7	na
1955	165.9	1,494.9	na
1960	180.7	1,665.3	87.5
1965	194.3	2,087.6	102.3
1970	205.1	2,416.2	120.5
1975	216.0	2,695.0	125.3
1980	227.7	3,187.1	142.6
1985	238.5	3,618.7	152.5
1990	250.0	4,155.8	167.4

Percent Increase:

Year	Population	GNP	Municipal Waste
1960–70	13.5	45	38
1970–80	11.0	32	18
1980–90	10.0	30	17
1960–90	39.0	150	91
1935–90	96.5	616	na

na = not available

Sources: U.S. Department of Commerce, Bureau of the Census, 1991, *Current Population Reports* (Washington, DC: GPO); Executive Office of the President, Council of Economic Advisors, 1991, *1991 Economic Report* Washington, DC: GPO); U.S. Environmental Protection Agency, Office of Solid Waste and Emergency Response, 1990, *Characterization of Municipal Solid Waste in the U.S., 1960–2000* (Prairie Village, KS: Franklin Associates).

economies, as a system based on maximizing profit, capitalism is inconsistent with maintaining environmental quality. The following chapters develop this theme in greater detail.

Conclusion

The tension between private rights and public rights fundamentally limits public policy options. On the one hand, liberalism's narrow concept of communal good places individual rights above communal claims. On the other hand, public life itself has become dominated by

TABLE 1.2. U.S. Energy Consumption 1960–1990 (Quadrillion Btu)

Year	Fossil Fuel Consumption	Total Energy Consumption
1960	29.7	43.8
1965	34.9	52.7
1970	41.8	66.4
1975	45.4	70.6
1980	49.6	76.0
1985	48.4	73.9
1990	53.4	81.17

Sources: U.S. Department of Energy, Energy Information Administration, 1989, *Annual Energy Review 1988* (Washington, DC: GPO); U.S. Department of Energy, Energy Information Administration, 1990, *Annual Energy Outlook 1990 with Projections to 2010* (Washington, DC: GPO); U.S. Department of Energy, Energy Information Administration, 1992, *International Energy Annual 1990* (Washington, DC: GPO).

TABLE 1.3 U.S. Timber Extraction and Pesticide Use 1960–1990

Year	Timber (billion cubic feet)	Pesticide Use (million pounds active ingredient)
1960	10.2	na
1964	11.2	291
1966	11.5	328
1971	11.5	464
1976	12.5	650
1982	14.2	552
1986	17.0	475
1987	17.7p	429
1988	17.9p	440
1989	17.7p	463
1990	17.9p	na

na = not available

p = preliminary

Sources: U.S. Department of Agriculture, Economic Research Service, periodic, *Inputs Outlook and Situation Report* (Washington, DC: GPO); U.S. Department of Agriculture, Forest Service, 1989, *1988 U.S. Timber Production, Trade Production, and Price Statistics* (Washington, DC: GPO).

private interests. As a result of this policy schizophrenia, American liberalism has limited mechanisms to confront issues that challenge individual interests on behalf of a notion of public good. Consequently, problems that affect communal resources, such as air and water, have little resolution within the traditional Liberal paradigm.

Furthermore, the policy process in the United States tends to favor large economic interests. Those interests that create the most damage to environmental resources—large industrial manufacturing plants, corporate agriculture, and mining interests—are best able to assemble the requisite political resources to influence the policy process.

When vague communal problems conflict with the specific rights of corporate individuals, Liberal policy stands with the latter. This occurs, not out of greed, but out of procedural necessity. There simply has been no structure to accommodate communal needs distinct from individual needs. As a result, policy makers have traditionally sought to ease communal problems without challenging the dominance of private rights.

Environmental policy is not the only issue area where these tensions exist. But, as a policy area directly concerned with the regulation of property use, environmental legislation provides an excellent case study of the contradictions within Liberal policy making. This chapter has outlined the theoretical framework of the discussion. Chapter 2 explores the role of symbolic politics in obfuscating the tension between liberalism and environmental quality. The remaining chapters explore these tensions within the specific environmental issue areas of air, water, waste, and energy. Chapter 8 explores the options facing Liberal society in the face of environmental challenges.

2 Symbolic Politics: Creating and Accommodating Public Demand

Chapter 1 asserted that liberal society has a limited capacity to resolve environmental problems as a result of its narrow definition of communal good and the expansionary character of its economic system. This chapter explores the role symbolic politics plays in easing the tension between liberalism and environmental quality. The manipulation of public opinion through symbolic policy is, perhaps, the strongest accommodation in the conflict between public and private rights. Such an accommodation allows Liberal society to retain the procedure of Democratic participation while eliminating the substance of Democratic accountability. As a result of the boundaries imposed by symbolic politics, the notion of Democratic choice is severely limited.

Symbolic Politics Defined

Politics can be understood as a function of hegemony and symbolic policy. Hegemony can be understood as the preponderant influence exercised by the dominant class in society (the elite). Gramsci (1935) defines hegemony as the "spontaneous consent" given by the mass of society to the influence "imposed on social life by the dominant fundamental group" (1935:12). This consent, Gramsci argues, is given as a result of the "prestige" the elite enjoy due to their social position. Hegemony is distinct, in Gramsci's view, from the coercive domination of the state:

> The apparatus of state coercive power . . . "legally" enforces discipline on those groups who do not "consent" either actively or passively. The apparatus is, however, constituted for the whole of society in anticipation of moments of crisis of command and direction when spontaneous consent has failed. (Gramsci 1935:12)

Symbolic politics, then, can be understood as one of the vehicles used to engineer spontaneous consent.

Edelman (1973; 1988) distinguishes between symbols that merely stand for something, such as a red traffic light (referential symbols), and symbols that condense both connotative and affective elements of some larger experience into a simple representation, such as the flag (condensational symbols):

> In the measure that anything serves as a condensational symbol, reactions to it are not based upon facts that are observed and that can be verified or falsified. Responses are based, rather, upon social suggestion: upon what others cue us to believe. (Edelman 1973:7)

Edelman echoes Adorno and his colleagues (1950) in pointing out that symbolic politics exists whenever a climate of ambiguity emerges:

> [The] combination of ambiguity and widespread public anxiety is precisely the climate in which people are eager for reassurance that they are being protected and therefore eager to believe that publicized governmental actions have the effects they are supposed to have. (Edelman 1973:12)

It is the need for reassurance that predisposes mass society to be vulnerable to symbolic representations of reality. Symbolic policy, then, is an effort by policy elites, who, through their social position or ability to marshall the requisite political resources, are able to manipulate public opinion and engineer consensus.

No one person can possibly experience the entire world. Yet everyone has an image or "picture" of the world. Burke (1966) suggests that however important that "sliver of reality each of us has experienced firsthand," the overall "picture" is a "construct of symbolic systems" (1966:5). This construct is based on political cognitions which are "ambivalent and highly susceptible to symbolic cues" (Edelman 1971:2). Government, Edelman argues, influences behavior by shaping the cognitions of people in ambiguous situations. In this way, government—or policy elites—helps engineer beliefs about what is "fact" and what is "proper" (Edelman 1971).

Several studies expose the ambiguous and often conflicting opinions most people have (e.g., Key 1961, Lane 1962, and Converse 1964). These cognitive inconsistencies make publics vulnerable to symbolic cues from government. Further, Edelman argues, the "eagerness to believe that government will ward off evils and threats renders [citizens] susceptible to political language" (1977).

The Engineering of Consent

Democracy is based on the notion of consent: through active participation citizens consent to be governed by the chosen body; citizens consent to the legitimacy of authority; and, ultimately, citizens consent to the outcomes of "democratic" government. In any political society, citizens undergo a systematic socialization process. It is both conscious and unconscious, incorporating a variety of socializing agents and resulting in specific outcomes. Family, school, the workplace, the media, the choreographed political process, social pressures, and cultural norms all prescribe specific values and attitude orientations. While different belief systems are identifiable within a society, the boundaries of the overall value system are very well defined.

Political socialization creates attitudes and opinions that, while different to some extent, converge in significant areas, establishing the boundaries of a values consensus. While there are few but significant pockets of critical opposition to the dominant consensus, these pockets are ineffective in gaining representation due to their small numbers, lack of unity, and ultimately an inability to wield political clout due to a lack of economic resources and social prestige. Further, political activities which challenge the dominant consensus are traditionally perceived as deviant behavior and are consequently suppressed with appropriate force. Political repression, such as the violent response to the Pullman strike of 1894, the use of National Guard troops against labor in the 1930s, the brutal state and local police response to civil rights organizers, J. Edgar Hoover's FBI and the red scare of the 1950s, and ultimately the violent response to anti–Vietnam War protests and government harassment of movement organizers, has consistently been defended as necessary governmental actions to protect domestic tranquility.

Political attitudes of the dominant consensus are translated into specific types of political behavior, all of which reinforce dominant political culture. Voting, campaign involvement, letter writing, and peaceful protest all reinforce Locke's notion of tacit consent. Citizen participation reinforces paternal agency and acknowledges the legitimacy of the political structure. Political participation obligates one to accept the outcome as the legitimate result of the democratic process. Edelman suggests:

> The political symbols that most powerfully inculcate support for the political system itself are those institutions we are taught to think of as the core of the democratic state: those that give people control over government. . . . Whatever else they accomplish, the holding of elections helps create a belief in the reality of political

participation in government and popular control over basic policy directions. . . . The belief is crucial whether or not it is accurate. (Edelman 1973:9–10)

In this sense symbolic politics accommodates the Democratic process. It allows Liberal society to retain procedural democracy, while limiting substantive discourse. Democratic politics presupposes a free exchange of ideas. Utilitarian theorists argued persuasively that truth is dependent upon the tension between conflicting views. Free speech, then, is a major foundation of Democratic politics, as it is the basis by which political choices are made. If speech is restricted to a narrow and symbolic context, the possibility of meaningful discourse is seriously limited.

Walter Lippmann (1922) considered the narrowing context of discourse reflected in the media as the "manufacture of consent." In *Public Opinion* Lippmann summed up the similar opinions a society would share:

A mass exposed to the same stimuli would develop responses that could theoretically be charted in a polygon of error. There would be a certain group that felt sufficiently alike to be classified together. There would be variants of feeling at both ends. These classifications would tend to harden as individuals in each of the classifications made their reactions vocal. That is to say, when the vague feelings of those who felt vaguely had been put into words, they would know more definitely what they felt, and would then feel it more definitely . . . Leaders in touch with popular feelings are quickly conscious of these reactions (1922:155–56).

As mass media have increasingly come to replace traditional agents of socialization, citizens have come to rely upon the selective slice of reality mass media represent. Consent, in Lippmann's model, is based on the acceptance of the selective reality constructed by policy makers and the mass media—upon which citizens base political attitudes, opinions, and, ultimately, action. Iyengar and Kinder's 1987 study supports this. They found that "by priming certain aspects of national life while ignoring others, television news sets the terms by which political judgments are rendered and political choices made" (Iyengar and Kinder 1987:4). Page and Shapiro (1992) are more specific. Their research suggests that policy elites consciously manipulate information in an effort to engineer the policy preferences of Americans.

The notion of creating consensus, of course, did not start with Lippmann. Plato's well-ordered utopia was based on the success of a civic education molding virtuous citizens. Machiavelli was equally concerned with consent, defining virtue (*virtu'*) as the ability of a prince to manufacture regime support. Lippmann simply brought the manufacture of consent into the technocratic age.

Since Lippmann, few scholars have explored explicitly the relationship between symbolic policy and consent.[1] This model of public policy moves away from elite conspiracy theories and focuses more on insights of political economists. Specifically, the political marketplace has as much to sell as the economic marketplace, and the same assumptions of creating consumers through marketing applies. Elites do not conspire to run the country. On the contrary, in pursuing their own self-interests, the line between selling cars and selling public policy is often blurred.

Symbolic Politics and Public Policy

Machiavelli described effectively how a prince might best maximize his power. The engineering of consensus is central in this process. In *Presidential Power*, Neustadt (1980) applies the lessons of *The Prince* to the contemporary American experience. Again, maximizing one's power through the manufacture of consent is paramount. Virtue, according to Machiavelli, is in controlling one's fortune. Political virtue is the ability to control the destiny of one's state. This, he points out, is best realized by the prince who, first and foremost, knows the art of war and gains the respect and adulation of his subjects. But, like Locke, Machiavelli relies on the consent of the governed whenever possible. His notion of citizen armies necessitates a positive relationship between the populace and the prince. Respect and adulation enable the prince to move effectively in making decisions. Yet Machiavelli keeps in mind that when all else fails, fear is the ultimate motivating force.

Machiavelli presents a blueprint for the effective development and maintenance of power. *Virtu'*, controlling destiny, is based on the successful manipulation of human circumstances. The virtuous prince is good, merciful, and honest, as long as expediency dictates. Yet he must be prepared to be cruel and deceptive. Control is the primary consideration, both of one's populace and of one's neighboring states. The republic is Machiavelli's ideal state, as he recognizes clearly the power of implicit consent inherent in limited democratic participation. Participation in political decisions, however limited, leads one to accept the outcome. But this participation is dependent upon the civic virtue of the population. The populace must be sufficiently civic-minded and free of corruption. Considering the difficulty of such a proposition, Machiavelli doubts that social dynamics can remain consistently virtuous. Consequently, the republic is only ideal to the extent that democratic participation can be suspended and political power centralized for effective control in periods of crisis. There is an awkward compatibility between democracy and autocracy in Machiavelli, as the populace could either be virtuous enough or scared enough to consent to a centralization of power.

Presidential *virtu'* is based in large part on the presentation of image. Every decision must take into account how it will be perceived. Since the president lacks the formal power of a dictator, he or she must rely upon, in Neustadt's terms, the power to persuade. The reputation of a president, and his or her future power, is dependent on a strong image. Charisma is essential for developing persuasive power, as the president must be respected and even loved. The president must act quickly and decisively to criticize opponents and reward allies. And, perhaps most important for both Machiavelli and Neustadt, the president must make effective use of the political climate. Only through the successful resolution of crisis can a president truly create dependence and power.

While Machiavelli's prince can rely upon respect or fear, presidents, for the most part, can only rely upon respect and the successful engineering of consent. Through deception and manipulation of the political climate, a president can essentially create consent. Favorable public opinion, Machiavelli's notion of adulation, is necessary for presidential action. Drawing on cultural biases, symbols, and traditions a skilled president can maximize his or her power (Edelman 1973; Cobb and Elder 1983a). Locke's notion of executive prerogative and the cunning of Machiavelli's prince each influence the successful American president. In this sense the marriage of Locke and Machiavelli becomes evident. Condensing complex realities into simplistic symbolic representations requires the careful reconstruction of events and the successful manipulation of cultural biases.

Reagan's invasion of Grenada in 1983, for example, was justified in large part by the administration's accusation that Grenada was undergoing "Cuban-Soviet Militarization." Reagan appeared on national television with a reconnaissance photograph purporting to show the construction of a Soviet air base. In fact, the photograph showed the construction of a commercial airport financed by U.S. allies, including Canada. Nonetheless, Reagan was successful in soliciting public support. The Bush administration, similarly, had systematically distorted intelligence reports on Iraqi intentions and military capabilities to increase support for the Gulf War (Royce 1991). Through the successful use of symbols and factual distortions, an effective president can pursue policies at his or her own discretion.

Examples of political marketing through symbolic language are plentiful. The official statement on the Grenada invasion was that "Caribbean Peace Keeping Forces" staged a "rescue mission" of American medical students with a "predawn vertical insertion" (Lutz 1989). The war in the Persian Gulf brought images of "smart bombs" "pacifying" enemy positions. In reality, only 7 percent of the bombs dropped were guided. Further, according to Air Force Gen. Merrill McPeak, of the 88,500 tons of explosives dropped on Iraq and occupied Kuwait, only 30 percent hit their targets (*Washington Post* 1991). Symbolic euphemisms such as "collateral damage," "friendly fire," and even "target rich environments" became adopted by the media and, in turn, the public. Through such choreography, the Defense Department and the State Department allowed citizens to participate in their own indoctrination.

Still, symbolic language need not be based on such obvious euphemisms and deceptions. On the contrary, most symbolic politics is a function of consciously oversimplifying complex realities into easily digestible political products that can then be sold by policy elites. Further, symbolic politics do not necessarily manufacture public demand as such. Organic public wants exist. In many cases, policy elites use symbolic action to cue the public into specific policy agendas. Earth Day, 1970, for example, was an outpouring of public concern over environmental degradation. Policy elites responded with policies that satisfied public demand but failed to resolve the environmental issues at hand. This was an example of, in Edelman's words, "words that succeed and policies that fail" (1977).

Mass Dependency and Symbolic Politics

Walter Lippmann redefined the manufacture of consent within the paradigm of the emerging mass media. While remaining true to its Machiavellian roots, the manufacture of consent in the technocratic age has become, Lippmann points out, even more insidious:

> That the manufacture of consent is capable of great refinements no one, I think, denies. . . . and the opportunities for manipulation open to anyone who understands the process are plain enough. . . . The creation of consent is . . . improved enormously in technic [sic], because it is now based on analysis rather than on rule of thumb. And so, as a result of psychological research, coupled with the modern means of communication, the practice of democracy has turned a corner. (1922:158)

If Machiavelli is correct in his dictum that a wise prince will maximize his power through deception, Lippmann's observations deserve consideration.

The manufacture of consent is distinct from political socialization in that it seeks not only to reproduce political values, but to manipulate public opinion to favor particular policies. While the relationship between public opinion and public policy may be a tenuous one, the perceived legitimacy of a regime is paramount for the maintenance of a stable political environment. In this sense, political socialization can be seen as setting the stage for later symbolic reinforcement. Easton writes:

> The inculcation of a sense of legitimacy is probably the single most effective device for regulating the flow of diffuse support in favor both of the authorities and of the regime. A member may be willing to obey the authorities and conform to the requirements of the regime for many different reasons. But the most stable support will derive from the conviction on the part of the member that it is right and proper for him to accept and obey the authorities and to abide by the requirements of the regime. It reflects the fact that in some way he sees these objects as conforming to his own moral principles, his own sense of what is right and proper in the political sphere. (1965:278)

Adorno and his colleagues (1950) argue that specific personality traits exist in citizens which make them susceptible to elite manipulation. The authors suggest that a psychological need exists among the mass for paternal leadership:

> [Propaganda] must . . . make its major appeal, not to rational self-interest, but to emotional needs—often the most primitive and irrational wishes and fears. . . . Why are [citizens] so easily fooled? . . . because of long-established patterns of hopes and aspirations, fears and anxieties that dispose them to certain beliefs and make them resistant to others. The task of fascist propaganda, in other words, is rendered easier to the degree that antidemocratic potentials already exist in the great mass of people. (Adorno, et al., 1950:10)

In short, citizens are vulnerable to a paternal and reassuring leader, a leader with simple answers that speak to their deepest anxieties. Effective elites will exploit these fears and anxieties in reaffirming regime ideology, which in turn legitimizes the elite issue agenda.

Pluralists may argue that the American experience is unique from the war-torn Europe that Adorno studied. American exceptionalism asserts that anti-Democratic tendencies in the American mass have been neutralized by consensus (e.g., Hartz 1955). This, however, overstates the case. Intolerance is widespread in the American psyche, albeit with a different cultural symbolism. Using tolerance of ideological nonconformity as the measure, Stouffer (1955) found that approximately two-thirds of Americans disagreed with the values expressed in the Bill of Rights. While this study is inherently limited due to the pervasive intolerance of the cold war era, later studies revealed similar findings. The study conducted by Nunn and colleagues (1973), using the same measures, found that approximately one-half of the population remained intolerant. The NORC General Social Surveys through 1980 found similar results. Considering the increasing level of education among the American population, continuing political intolerance presents an irony. Yet, in reinforcing the legitimacy of competitive liberalism, public education may play a fundamental role in maintaining political intolerance.

These studies expose abstract fears and values that exist within the populace. Elite success in manipulating these anxieties depends, in large part, on the issue agenda, as this agenda defines the questions upon which these fears, anxieties, and values are applied. As Lippmann and Neustadt suggest, the content of the issue agenda defines the policy areas to be addressed. Consequently, agenda building is central in establishing consent. That is, effective elites will define the issue agenda so as to focus on the questions that best suit their goals. This will include "easy," emotionally laden symbolic issues which attract citizen attention, as well as specific policy issues that require mass support (Cobb and Elder 1983b). Edelman suggests that effective elites will arouse anxiety in order to quell it (1977).

There are, of course, limits to the success of symbolic politics. Effectiveness depends upon a credible voice articulating an easily digestible agenda to a public atmosphere of ambiguity and anxiety. To the extent opinion cues contradict widespread personal experience, symbolic action will be less effective. Environmental policy is an arena where personal experience and symbolic cues have come together. The following section explores how the environmental issue is ripe for symbolic manipulation.

Symbolic Politics and Environmental Policy

The environmental debate is permeated with ambiguity and anxiety. It is, simultaneously, a "hard" and "easy" issue (Carmines and Stimson

1981). On the one hand, environmental improvement is a highly specialized technical field encompassing physicists, chemists, geologists, engineers, physicians, economists, and other experts. Specific regulatory proposals, consequently, are beyond most people's grasp. This results in two dynamics: most people lose interest in the specifics of the environmental debate; and, those who remain interested are often shut out from participation due to a lack of expertise.

On the other hand, environmental quality remains a highly salient issue with the public. "Clean air" and "clean water" emerge as emotional issues through which many people develop a passionate desire for environmental improvement. As a consequence, the public is vulnerable to simplistic answers and symbolic explanations. The problem, of course, is that there are no simple or easy answers to the crisis in environmental quality.

The original Earth Day in April 1970 is a good illustration of a passionate public (high issue salience) with little long-term commitment (low issue strength). Citizens came together across the country and demanded, in somewhat vague terms, environmental improvement. In the months following Earth Day, public enthusiasm waned. This dynamic was identified by Downs (1972) as the issue-attention cycle, whereby mass public support would push the environmental issue to the top of the formal political agenda. Ultimately, Downs saw a five-stage model. Initially, experts and advocates recognize a problem (preproblem stage). Some crisis brings the issue to the attention of the mass public (euphoric enthusiasm stage). Then as the public comes to realize the costs of solving the problem, public support softens. Ultimately, there is a decline in the intense public interest. Finally, the issue moves into "a twilight realm of lesser attention or spasmodic recurrences of interest" (post-problem stage) (Downs 1972:39–40, in Dunlap 1989:89). This process of issue replacement may have been helped by what Jones (1974) calls public satisfying policy. The Clean Air Act of 1970, Jones argues, sought to satisfy public demand for strong environmental policy. However, when the deadlines of the act were continually extended, little public outcry was heard.

The ambiguous and anxious climate surrounding environmental quality creates the desire, on the part of the public, for quick resolution. The complexity of the policy arena makes public opinion vulnerable to charismatic leaders promising solutions to the crisis (Adorno, et al., 1950; Edelman 1977). Neustadt (1980) reminds us that wise policy elites will maximize their interests by exploiting the vulnerabilities with which they are confronted. This is often played out by a policy maker who reduces a complex problem into a simple symbolic representation.

In the context of environmental regulation, policy makers have sought to resolve the tension between economic interests and public demand for environmental improvement through "symbolic politicking." This has taken four forms, as the following chapters outline in greater detail. First, the policy discourse on environmental quality has minimized the extent of the problem. Second, the costs of comprehensive pollution controls have been distorted. Third, the costs of environmental degradation already borne by citizens has largely been ignored. And fourth, the effectiveness of limited policy alternatives has consistently been exaggerated.

Conclusion

Contemporary public policy is permeated with ambiguity, and often anxiety. Environmental quality, especially, is an arena of complex problems, conflicting interests, and confusing solutions. As a consequence, environmental policy is often characterized by discourse that seeks to satisfy public anxiety while maintaining a commitment to traditional Liberal economic development. The Clean Air Act, the Clean Water Act, and the several acts addressing solid and hazardous waste each offer limited contributions to environmental quality. Yet the regulations fall far short of fulfilling their stated claims.

The following chapters explore these issues in greater detail, focusing on the substantive areas within the environmental policy arena.

3 The Environmental
Policy Subsystem

Environmental quality is a particularly difficult arena of public policy. It challenges the very core of Liberal theory: private rights to property, free of communal regulation. This chapter defines the evaluative criteria used throughout the study and establishes the parameters of the environmental policy subsystem. Further, the chapter explores the role bureaucratic politics plays in symbolic action. Specifically, procedural manipulation provides a vehicle for bypassing regulatory statutes, allowing policy elites to claim policy success while simultaneously inhibiting policy implementation.

Evaluative Criteria

Environmental policy has traditionally been evaluated by four criteria: (1) achieving specific environmental quality goals or standards (outcomes evaluation); (2) the cost-effectiveness of achieving these goals (benefit-cost analysis); (3) public support of the policies; and (4) success in resolving political conflicts that may be created by regulation (Marcus 1986). The 1970 Clean Air Act added a "scientific" criterion, requiring that air quality standards be developed without regard to cost. Reagan's executive order 12291 instituted a purely economic criterion, stating that all policies administered by executive agencies be implemented only when "potential benefits to society outweigh potential costs to society." "Costs" are narrowly defined in economic terms, while "benefits" remain vague.

This study argues that environmental policy is more effectively evaluated when criteria are based on a more general concept of fulfilling human needs. Public policy, after all, is the effort by society to deal with human needs. While economic development is a necessary component of contemporary society, it is not the only component. Thus, using a purely economic calculus to determine policy efficaciousness has the effect of removing policy from its human base. Human needs are best served when environmental quality standards are established according to scientific data concerned with sustaining public health and in sustaining natural resources. Public policies are more likely to meet the needs of society when they address the holistic spectrum of human concerns, including health, resource management, aesthetics, and economics. Finally, any evaluation of environmental policy success must include an analysis of implementation and of compliance with established regulations.

There are several differences these criteria have with existing criteria. First, economic cost alone is a poor indicator of policy efficaciousness. While economic health has an impact on public health, toxic materials and depleted resources represent a greater threat to health. Policies that favor compromising public health in favor of economic growth are inherently flawed and shortsighted. Second, if a benefit-cost calculation is employed it must account for the broader costs society is already paying as a result of environmental degradation: rising frequencies of illness in urban areas; lost productivity as a consequence of this absenteeism; pollution-related property degradation; and a net deficit in resource availability, including clean air, drinkable groundwater, arable soil, timber and forest resources, and energy resources.

Environmental degradation is troublesome because although it represents a threat to human survival, the degree of that threat is difficult to measure. We simply do not know how much environmental damage the earth can absorb and still sustain life. As such, the environmental threat is a contested terrain. Those who argue that "unemployment is bad for your health," and thus environmental policy should be restricted from interfering with economic growth, ignore the crucial difference between economics and environmental quality. Economics determines resource production and allocation. But, resource distribution need not be left to the vagaries of the "market"; alternate distribution systems have been successfully used in times of austerity—World War II, for example. On the other hand, environmental resources are largely static. They exist in limited supply, and once destroyed may never be replaced.

In evaluating policy success, this study explores five issues: (1) the strength of environmental quality goals and standards using public health and resource management as policy priorities; (2) policy timetables and deadlines; (3) implementation success and compliance; (4) lifestyle changes aimed at improving environmental quality; and (5) alternative technologies aimed at reducing degradation and improving environmental quality. Before going directly into the substantive issue areas, the following section reviews the evolution and structure of the environmental policy subsystem.

The Evolution of a National Environmental Policy

Concern for the natural environment is not new. The systematic drive for environmental protection through legislation has evolved through the efforts of movements which trace their roots back to the nineteenth century. As early as the 1860s, the need for sustaining forest resources was broadly discussed. Basic forest preservation was introduced through limited forest reserves in 1891 and selective cutting programs in 1897 (Caulfield 1989). In tracing the evolution of environmental regulation from conservationism in the 1860s to the passage of the National Environmental Protection Act (NEPA) in 1969, this section explores the evolution of the environmental policy bureaucracy.

The appearance of preservationism as distinct from traditional conservationism emerged during the presidency of Theodore Roosevelt. Conservationists have traditionally sought the development and regulation of natural resources, to ensure long-term resource extraction. On the other hand, the emerging preservationist movement sought to protect specific resources by banning development and resource extraction altogether. It was the preservationist movement that was responsible for setting aside Yosemite Valley as a state park in 1860 (designated as a national park in 1890), as well as for the creation of Yellowstone National Park in 1872.

The preservationist movement began in the west. Led by the San Francisco–based Sierra Club (established in 1892 by John Muir), preservationists met stiff resistance from ranching and mining interests who favored conservationists, but managed to win the creation of the National Park Service in 1916. This was significant because it allowed for the transfer of public land from the Forest Service, a strictly conservationist agency, to the Park Service, an agency whose mandate was to preserve public lands. By the 1940s and 1950s public sentiment was strong enough to allow Congress to pass the federal water protection acts over the vetoes of presidents Truman and Eisenhower. And, by 1961, the Senate Select Committee on National Water Resources sought federal plain regulation as an alternative to flood-control dams (Caulfield 1989).

The contemporary environmental movement coincided with the "new politics" of the Kennedy administration, bringing together preservationists and those concerned with the degrading urban environment. In his "Special Message to the Congress on Natural Resources," Kennedy articulated a concern with depleting resources. The message outlined the need for federal legislation protecting air, water, forests, topsoil, wildlife, seashores, and public lands for recreational use. Kennedy's secretary of the interior, Stewart Udall, became the administration's environmental torchbearer. He sought an increase in federal parklands, ordered the Fish and Wildlife Service to draft an endangered species act, and by 1964 turned the dull annual reports of the Interior Department into unusually colorful publications with a wide readership. Udall himself traveled the country giving speeches on behalf of his preservationist policies.

While President Johnson's concern for the environment is perhaps popularly known only as highway beautification projects, he remained sensitive to the growing environmental constituency. In September 1964 the Land and Water Conservation Fund Act and the Wilderness Act were signed into law. The Water Quality Act establishing the Federal Water Pollution Control Administration was signed in 1965. The first Clean Air Act was adopted in 1965, and the Air Quality Act in 1967. The Endangered Species Act was signed in 1966 (and a revised act in 1969). Finally, in October 1968, Johnson signed the Wild and Scenic Rivers Act and the National Trails System Act, and established the North Cascades National Park and Redwood National Park (Caulfield 1989).

Nixon's election to office slowed the early environmental momentum. His appointment to secretary of interior was Walter Hickel, a former governor of Alaska who was more concerned with development than with environmental protection. In order to satisfy the Senate Interior Committee, Nixon ultimately appointed Russell Train, president of the Conservation Foundation, as under-secretary of the interior. Though Nixon was by no means an environmentalist, he was not prepared to fight a Congress aware of the growing environmental concern among the public. Hesitantly, the Nixon administration carried on the policies of his predecessors.

In an effort to bypass the legislative proposal for a National Environmental Protection Act (NEPA), Nixon created the Council on Environmental Quality (CEQ) (1969). Congress adopted NEPA anyway, and Nixon signed the bill into law. NEPA was the first comprehensive federal legislation aimed at protecting environmental resources. It requires environmental impact statements for evaluating all federal programs and formalized the Council on Environmental Quality in statutory law.

The growing strength of the grassroots environmental movement in the late 1960s came as a result of increasing urban pollution and numerous environmental mishaps, including the massive Santa Barbara oil spill in 1969. With the waning urgency of the anti–Vietnam War movement, much of the energy of the counter-culture was retained by the growing environmental movement. Popular concern culminated on Earth Day (1970), observed on university campuses throughout the country. Earth Day was a celebration of the nurturance and beauty of the natural environment and a day of education focusing on the difficult issues of environmental degradation. This growing salience was illustrated in the popularity of a number of books that held broad appeal, including Rachel Carson's *Silent Spring* (1962), Paul Erlich's *The Population Bomb* (1968), Charles Reich's *The Greening of America* (1970), and Barry Commoner's *The Closing Circle—Man, Nature, and Technology* (1971).

Clearly, the environmental issue had become a permanent feature on the national agenda. The resulting public demand for environmental improvement created a flood of legislation that went far beyond the incrementalism that had traditionally characterized environmental regulation. These policies, however, went further in satisfying an aroused public than in fulfilling stated policy claims. The following sections explore the environmental policy bureaucracy itself, with its conflicting jurisdictions and competing interests.

The Environmental Policy Web

The complexity of environmental regulation is exacerbated by the confusing web of federal departments, agencies, and committees that make up the environmental policy bureaucracy. This is a result, in part, of the incremental evolution of environmental policy. Prior to the establishment of the Environmental Protection Agency (EPA) as an executive agency in 1970, environmental policy was largely disconnected, spread out among numerous departments and agencies.

Within the executive office of the president, the Council on Environmental Quality had overseen environmental policy coordination, environmental quality reporting, and NEPA. It was replaced by president Clinton with the White House Environmental Policy Office in early 1993. The EPA oversees air and water pollution policy, pesticide control, radiation, solid waste, and toxic and hazardous waste (Superfund). The Nuclear Regulatory Commission (NRC) is responsible for regulating and licensing nuclear power industries. Cabinet-level departments are each responsible for maintaining the environmental integrity of programs within their respective jurisdictions. The Department of the Interior oversees public lands (Bureau of Land Management), energy, minerals, and national parks (National Park Service). The Department of Agriculture oversees forestry (Forest Service) and soil conservation. The Department of Commerce oversees oceanic and atmospheric monitoring and research. The State Department oversees international environmental agreements. The Justice Department is responsible for pursuing litigation for violations of environmental regulations. The Defense Department is responsible for pollution control of defense facilities and oversees civil works construction and dredge and fill permits (Army Corps of Engineers). The Energy Department oversees energy policy coordination and gas and oil research and development. The Department of Transportation oversees mass transit, roads, aerial noise pollution, and oil pollution (e.g., spills). The Department of Housing and Urban Development oversees urban parks and urban planning. The Department of Health and Human Services is responsible for health-related issues. Finally, the Labor Department is responsible for protecting occupational health. (Vig and Kraft 1990b) Clinton has stated his intention of elevating EPA to a cabinet-level department (Abramson 1993).

This web of environmental bureaus, agencies, and commissions creates a complex relationship. It is the vastness of the environmental bureaucracy that is its vulnerability. The conventional notion of an iron triangle—the cozy policy relationship between congressional subcommittees, regulatory agencies, and interest groups—is insufficient to explain the environmental-policy web. Rather, the complexity of the environmental bureaucracy, with so many competing regulatory and policy agencies, allows several points of policy manipulation. Traditional interest groups and PACs seek to influence each agency involved. Executive agencies seek to influence each other and congress. Congressional subcommittees lobby each other. And, in this competitive policy environment, back-door influence is sought through the Office of Management and Budget (OMB), which establishes the administration's policy priorities and maintains oversight on every regulatory agency.

Manipulating bureaucratic politics is, in itself, a form of symbolic politics. Procedural manipulation has allowed regulators to weaken or bypass regulatory statutes by failing to implement policies consistently. This, in turn, has allowed policy elites to satisfy public demand for environmental policy by pointing to the statutory existence of specific regulations, while at the same time allowing implementation to fall far short. The section below illustrates the symbolic aspect of bureaucratic stonewalling.

Symbolic Politics in Bureaucratic Policy Making

The age of reason brought promises of rational government, where bureaucratic consistency was to replace the arbitrary actions of petty despots. But bureaucratic government, with its vast hierarchies, invited a different form of administrative capriciousness. Individuals or offices within the bureaucracy are able to weaken or prevent implementation of policies simply by failing to follow through with systemic responsibilities.

Weber (1922) defined bureaucratic organization as a specific hierarchy of offices, each with a specialized task to do, with each task specifically defined. Weber's hierarchy is somewhat pyramidic, with authority diffused as one moves down the bureaucratic ladder. Lower offices, according to Weber, are not subservient to higher offices as such. Rather, all offices are subservient to the rule of law. To the extent that higher offices interpret law and establish policy, lower offices are subject to supervision. But these offices are, in Weber's view, protected from arbitrary intrusion.

When considering the environmental policy web, Weber's notion of a rational bureaucracy is accurate only in part. While bureaucratic organization is the only effective way to implement nationwide programs, such organization is vulnerable to manipulation. Weber's assumption that everyone within the bureaucracy would share the ideology of the bureaucratic culture is inaccurate. In fact, there is often serious disagreement as to the goals of the agency (Cahn and Kamieniecki 1993).

Like any policy process, there are resources that help to maximize one's power within the bureaucracy. The basic resources necessary for administrative power are knowledge, access, and charismatic leadership (Neustadt 1980; Rourke 1984). Knowledge is necessary in two respects. Knowledge of the bureaucratic process allows one to navigate through the various offices and agencies responsible for environmental policy. And, technical expertise is necessary to make decisions in complicated areas. Access to agency administrators is not ensured, and, consequently, one's ability to gain access is crucial in acquiring bureaucratic influence. Charismatic leadership may allow an administrator to mobilize support and loyalty among the agency staff. And, equally important, one's ability to mobilize support among peers within the bureaucracy may similarly influence the procedural agenda.

With the maze of agencies and departments that oversee various aspects of the environmental bureaucracy, environmental policy is especially vulnerable to manipulation. To protect against this, a number of mechanisms were set in place. The EPA was specifically developed with a proenvironment bias to preclude allowing regulated industries from "capturing" the agency. Another tool is the "administrative hammer" (Rosenbaum 1989). Hammer clauses ensure that policy is carried out the way Congress intended by including such mechanisms as explicit deadlines for implementation, requiring citizen participation, and extending legal standing to citizens allowing the public to bring suit against agencies if policies are not carried through, making it increasingly difficult for agency administrators to delay or pigeonhole policy objectives. Other barriers include specific statutory language that would ban members of the regulated industry from serving within the agencies. The Surface Mining Control and Reclamation Act (1977), for example, includes a clause that prohibits the Office of Surface Mining Reclamation and Enforcement (OSM) from hiring anyone who previously worked with any federal agency involved with the development of coal or any other mineral resources (PL 95–87, 1977; Rosenbaum 1989:214).

Yet such protection is not always enough. The environmental commitment that evolved through the 1960s and 1970s shifted fundamentally with the election of Ronald Reagan. For the first time agency administrators were unabashedly defiant in enforcing environmental regulation. Reagan's appointment of James Watt as secretary of interior and Anne (Gorsuch) Burford as administrator of the EPA effectively brought twenty years of environmental progress to a standstill.

Watt was the president of the Mountain States Legal Foundation, a corporate law firm in Denver that specialized in bringing suit against government regulations on behalf of prodevelopment interests. Eleven of Watt's top sixteen Interior officials were previously associated with the industries regulated by Interior: oil, mining, timber, livestock, and utilities (Kenski and Ingram 1986). The primary goal of the Interior Department under Watt was the easing of regulations on development of public lands. Specifically, Watt sought to accelerate energy and mineral extraction on federal lands, including the opening of national parks (McCurdy 1986). Within his first month as interior secretary, he announced plans to open almost all federal offshore waters to gas and oil company exploration. After strong bipartisan opposition from California, Watt offered a revised plan that still called for opening nearly 90 percent of northern California waters (Christensen and Gerston 1988). Although the Interior Department had been concerned with preserving environmental resources since Udall in the early 1960s, its traditional role had been much closer to resource development. It was, consequently, fairly easy for Watt to bring his agenda into the department.

The Environmental Protection Agency, on the other hand, had a different notion of its goals. Anne Burford brought the Reagan administration's philosophy of deregulation to the agency. A former Colorado legislator, Burford was a corporate attorney whose clients were generally hostile to environmental regulation. As EPA administrator, she sought to reduce regulatory standards in all areas. In order to sidestep the proenvironment culture that had been bred in the agency since Ruckelshaus, Burford instituted a number of procedural changes. One method was simply to hold unannounced meetings when discussing policy with regulated industries. The lack of public notice successfully precluded public comment (Rosenbaum 1985). In addition, Burford centralized all decision making in her office, effectively paralyzing staff activities (Cohen 1986). Burford initiated "political criteria" into the release of program money (Rosenbaum 1985). This was most evident in Rita Lavelle's refusal to release a large Superfund award to clean up the Stringfellow site in California. As director of the Office of Toxic Substances within EPA, Lavelle flatly rejected her legislative responsibility. The Stringfellow site was among the most dangerous hazardous waste sites in the country. Burford and Lavelle withheld the money, hoping to slow the cleanup and thereby make then California governor and Senate candidate Jerry Brown look ineffective (Rosenbaum 1985).

The Reagan administration applied heavy pressure on the EPA. The Office of Management and Budget (OMB), which oversees all policy implementation, pushed the EPA to revise existing regulations. This "backdoor influence" allowed the OMB to become a partner in regulatory decision making, without formally or publicly identifying with the agency. Such influence had the effect of reinterpreting congressional intent without actually altering legislation (Rosenbaum 1985). Under Reagan and Burford the EPA suffered severe budget cuts, reorganization of staff, and policy changes that effectively reversed many previous advances. Between 1980 and 1983 staff was cut from over eleven thousand to just over nine thousand, and EPA's non-Superfund budget was cut by 12 percent (Cohen 1986). After suffering severe credibility problems, Reagan pressed Burford to resign and reappointed William Ruckelshaus, the agency's first administrator under Nixon. The demoralized staff celebrated Burford's departure with eight cases of champagne (Rosenbaum 1985:56).

While the Bush administration was superior to Reagan's in the area of environmental quality, Bush remained closely aligned with industry. Within the OMB, Vice-President Quayle chaired the Council on Competitiveness, a little-known committee that reviewed, and often killed, regulations that had been developed and approved by independent regulatory agencies and cabinet-level departments. Under the premise of protecting America's "competitiveness" from overly burdensome regulations, the council served as a nonjudicial means for industry to challenge regulations.

More traditional procedural posturing also continued under Bush. Bush had promised to appoint an "environmentalist" to head the EPA during the 1988 campaign. Reilly, as president of World Wildlife Fund and Conservation Foundation, fit this description. As a middle-of-the-road environmentalist, Reilly sought increased cooperation between environmental regulators and industry (Amy 1990). As a consequence, critics have argued that Reilly may have gone too far in appeasing business interests. An illustrative case involves an EPA panel established to explore the health effects of secondary cigarette smoke. Seven of the sixteen panel members appointed had direct ties to the cigarette industry. Six worked with the Center for Indoor Air Research, a research center financed by the Philip Morris Company, R. J. Reynolds Tobacco, and the Lorrillard Corporation. The seventh was appointed to the EPA panel on the direct recommendation of Philip Morris. While the presence of tobacco-industry-sponsored researchers on the secondary-cigarette-smoke panel did little to sway the panel away from the conclusion that secondary smoke is responsible for thirty-eight-hundred lung cancer deaths every year, the conflict of interest is apparent. The cigarette industry has criticized the study as "incomplete and unreliable" (Associated Press 1990b; *Los Angeles Times* 1990).

The appointment of William Reilly as EPA administrator was widely seen as a gesture to the environmental community. And, although Reilly's appointment helped to raise morale within the agency, Bush refused to allow the budget and staff increases necessary to fully recover from the Burford years (Vig 1990). This was not surprising. Bush's nominees to other environmentally related agencies were clearly hostile to environmental issues. Bush's director of the Bureau of Land Management (BLM) was Delos Jamison, a former employee of James Watt. The director of the National Park Service was James Ridenour, an associate of Dan Quayle and a former fundraiser for the Republican party. Bush's appointee to head the Forest Service was James Cason, who as acting assistant secretary for land and minerals management sought the opening of national parks and wilderness areas to strip mining and oil drilling (Vig 1990:49). Cason failed to be confirmed by the Senate.

The Clinton administration represents a significant departure from the Reagan-Bush years. Clinton's selection of Al Gore as vice-president gave environmentalists optimism. Gore's book *Earth in the Balance* (1992) calls for civilization to "restore the balance" between human needs and environmental needs. Clinton's EPA administrator, Carol Browner, has a positive record as head of Florida's Department of Environmental Regulation (Kenworthy 1992). Clinton's secretary of interior, Bruce Babbitt, was president of the League of Conservation Voters and has a strong environmental record as governor of Arizona (Kenworthy 1993).

Still, there are several troubling indicators. Clinton's appointment of Hazel O'Leary as secretary of energy stirred concern among many. O'Leary was executive vice-president for corporate affairs for Northern States Power Company, one of the nation's most powerful utilities. While at Northern States Power, O'Leary came under criticism for her public disputes with regulators over the disposition of nuclear waste from the company's three nuclear power plants (Lippman 1993). Clinton's replacement of the Council on Environmental Quality with the White House Office of Environmental Policy has received the endorsement of mainstream environmental organizations. But the new office is significantly smaller than the CEQ, and the administrator, while energetic and committed, is young and inexperienced, and therefore at a severe disadvantage when competing with the National Security Council, the National Economic Council, or the Domestic Policy Council for policy priorities (Abramson 1993). Finally, the Clinton administration has been unusually slow in making regulatory appointments. By September, after ten months in office, the administration had not been able to get a single EPA national program manager confirmed by the Senate and only one of the ten EPA regional administrators had been appointed (Piasecki 1993). Clinton's first-year priorities have clearly been elsewhere.

Clinton's success in getting the North American Free Trade Agreement (NAFTA) ratified has split the environmental community. Groups such as the World Wildlife Fund and the Natural Resources Defense Council have endorsed NAFTA, arguing that the trade agreement and its environmental side agreements will provide an international mechanism for addressing environmental degradation. Others, such as the Sierra Club, have opposed NAFTA, arguing that it will be used to challenge U.S. environmental laws as restraints to trade. According to the agreement, the United States would be obliged to scuttle domestic laws that may be deemed inconsistent with the agreement (Benson 1993). Such laws might include air and water regulations, pesticide controls, wildlife protection, recycling programs, and energy laws. While Clinton may have a sincere interest in improving environmental quality, his policy priorities, like those of his predecessors, focus on economic growth. The NAFTA debate illustrates the tensions between economic issues, such as free trade, and environmental regulation.

The manipulation of the environmental policy bureaucracy is a form of symbolic politics. While the Reagan administration was claiming success in improving environmental quality, it succeeded in slowing environmental enforcement to a snail's pace. Reagan's perception of an "electoral mandate" for "regulatory relief" allowed the administration to sidestep policy implementation through severe budget cuts and the institution of a narrow cost-benefit criterion in evaluating policy efficaciousness. Similarly, Bush continued to lay claim to the environmental camp through the end of his failed 1992 campaign. Symbolic claims of policy success allowed the administration to mollify public demand, while procedural manipulation blocked policy implementation. Clinton, on the other hand, has given environmental concerns rhetorical consideration, but has thus far offered little in the way of substantive policy.

Conclusion

This chapter discussed the evaluative criteria the study uses to determine policy efficaciousness. They include: the strength of mandated standards, using public health and resource management as policy priorities; rigor of timetables and deadlines; implementation and compliance; lifestyle changes; and alternative technologies. Further, the chapter defined the parameters of the environmental policy subsystem. Finally, the chapter discussed the bureaucratic implementation of environmental policy and the vulnerabilities that allow procedural manipulation of policy implementation. The following chapters explore the specific environmental policy issue areas, focusing on the tension between liberalism and environmental quality and the symbolic politics that have helped ease that tension.

4 Clean Air Policy

This legislation isn't just the centerpiece of our environmental agenda. It is simply the most significant air-pollution legislation in our nation's history . . . [we are entering] a new era for clean air.
—George Bush on the 1990 Clean Air Act, November 15, 1990

Clean air is a special concern for most people. In addition to the inherent life-giving quality of oxygen, clean air provides an aesthetic element necessary for a high quality of life. For centuries fresh air has been recognized for its invigorating appeal. Urban vacationers have always sought to get out into "the country." Parents push their children to get out and play in the fresh air. In a sense, access to clean air has been an important indicator of "the good life." As such, clean air is inherently symbolic. The increasing pollution brought by expanding industry and growing urbanization through the 1940s, 1950s, and 1960s raised public concern and anxiety. This concern culminated in Earth Day (1970) with the mobilization of mass public demand for strong environmental regulation.

Policy makers, recognizing the symbolic importance of clean air, sought to satisfy public demand with bold legislation in the Clean Air Act of 1970. Unfortunately, the promises of the act were never realized. The standards and deadlines of the act were sufficiently strict so as to preclude any realistic expectation of compliance. Ultimately, it succeeded in pacifying a demanding public and putting off the clean air debate until a later time when the public might be less mobilized.

This chapter examines air pollution control in light of the problem of communal good and the tension between capitalism and clean air. Ultimately, the chapter argues that the tension is eased through symbolic politics in the Clean Air Acts of 1970 and 1990. The chapter begins by examining the content and consequences of air pollution.

Background: The Content and Consequences of Air Pollution

In 1990 an estimated 134 million metric tons of airborne pollutants were emitted in the United States (EPA 1990). That is approximately twelve hundred pounds of soot, sulfur and nitrogen oxides, hydrocarbons, carbon monoxide, and lead for each American. Air pollution is a fact of industrial life. Whether it be driving a car, lighting a barbecue, or simply turning on a light switch in our homes, each of us contributes to the problem. Air pollution has four main causes. As the population has grown, urbanization has created densely populated cities resulting in a greater release of pollutants. The growing reliance on individual forms of transportation (e.g., automobiles) since World War II is a major contributor of airborne pollutants. The growth of industrialization has resulted in more industries spewing more pollutants. And the increasing demand for energy has resulted in the need for more and more utilities, most of which are fueled by coal and diesel, creating more emissions. Air pollution is not a new problem, the first antipollution law was passed in Chicago in 1881 prohibiting the emission of dense smoke from any smokestack within the city. Nonetheless, air pollution remains one of the most divisive issues confronting policy makers.

The issue has traditionally been problematic due to the mobility of airborne pollutants. Throughout the country, remnants of early air pollution controls are still visible. Smokestacks were simply built taller and taller, so as to deposit pollutants into the prevailing winds where they would be carried out of the area. Since air pollutants are mobile, communities have been hesitant to deal with the problem. The local emphasis that characterized early regulatory policy made it difficult for downwind communities to have any say in regulation of the pollution source. Even today, San Bernardino suffers through unhealthful and hazardous air as a result of its proximity to Los Angeles (Kamieniecki, Cahn, and Goss 1991).

The EPA has identified seven major elements of air pollution: carbon monoxide (CO); hydrocarbons (HC); lead (Pb); nitrogen dioxide (NO_2); ozone (O_3); particulate matter (PM); and sulfur dioxide (SO_2). Each of these components represents considerable health risks.

Carbon monoxide is emitted from vehicle and stationary source exhaust. It is an odorless gas that replaces oxygen in red blood cells. It can cause angina, impaired vision, poor coordination, and dizziness. While the earth releases CO naturally, the expansive release of industrial CO emissions contributes to the greenhouse effect, potentially throwing off the equilibrium of the earth's temperature balance (global warming).

Hydrocarbons, or volatile organic compounds, are released by the incomplete combustion of gasoline and evaporation from petroleum based fuels, solvents, and paints. Hydrocarbons react in the sunlight with oxygen and nitrogen dioxide to form ozone, peroxyacetyl nitrate (PAN), and other photochemical oxidants.

Ozone, the main component of smog, irritates the mucous membranes (eyes, nasal passages, throat, lungs) causing coughing, choking, and reduced lung capacity, as well as aggravating asthma, bronchitis, and emphysema. Smog, containing hundreds of chemicals, including ozone and peroxyacetyl nitrate, damages trees, crops, and building materials.

Lead is used as an antiknock additive in some gasolines, as well as a stabilizing agent in household and industrial paints, and a structural component of pipes and roofing. Nonferrous smelters and battery plants also emit lead into the atmosphere. Lead, like other heavy metals, accumulates in the fat, bone, and other soft tissues of the body. The most common symptoms of lead poisoning include nausea and severe stomach pains. Larger accumulations cause deterioration of blood-forming organs, kidneys, and ultimately the nervous system. As well, lead has been tied to learning disabilities in young children.

Nitrogen dioxide is a product of industrial and vehicle exhaust. It attacks the lungs, causing cellular changes resulting in lowered resistance to respiratory infections. NO_2 is a main contributor to acid rain, and when mixed with hydrocarbons it creates ozone, as discussed above.

Particulate matter is the smoke, dust, and soot that is emitted from industrial processes, heating boilers, gasoline and diesel engines, coal and diesel-burning utilities, cigarette smoke, and both organic and synthetic dusts. Larger particulates clog the lung sacs, causing bronchitis and more serious pneumoconioses (diseases related to inhalation of organic and inorganic dusts); irritate mucous membranes; and clog tear ducts, damaging the surface of the eye. Microscopic particulates pass into the bloodstream, introducing carcinogens and heavy metals (Price and Wilson 1986).

Sulfur dioxide is released in coal- and oil-burning processes. SO_2 is a corrosive, poisonous gas that is associated with coughing, colds, asthma, and bronchitis, and, like nitrogen dioxide, contributes to acid rain.

At best, airborne pollutants significantly reduce the capacity of the human immune system to protect the body from organic and inorganic poisons, viruses, and bacteria. At worst, these pollutants cause life debilitating diseases, such as cancer. As well, airborne pollutants have an impact beyond the damage caused by direct contact. Acid rain, global warming, and ozone depletion are consequences of air pollution. Each has a specific impact on environmental quality. Acid rain is a result of sulfur and nitrogen oxides combining with moisture in the air. Any precipitation (rain, snow, fog) brings the acidic moisture into contact with global resources. Forests, lakes and rivers, water tables, buildings, even bridges and train tracks are all damaged.

Acidity is measured on a pH scale, ranging from zero (most acidic) to fourteen (most alkaline). The pH scale is logarithmic, with each unit representing a tenfold increase. Distilled water has a pH level of seven. Clean rainwater has a pH level of between five and six. Battery acid has a pH level of one, lemon juice of two. In the most densely populated areas of the United States and Europe, acid levels of rain average a pH level of four. On rare occasions acid levels have been found to be as high as a pH of two (Corson 1990). Acid rain is capable of lowering pH levels of lakes so significantly that they can no longer support most life forms. Thousands of lakes in the eastern United States are incapable of supporting fish, and 10 percent of the lakes in the Adirondacks have a pH level below five. Furthermore, increased acidity causes soil, vegetation, and forest damage. There is already significant damage to coniferous trees, which are especially vulnerable to acid precipitation, throughout the Appalachian range from West Virginia to Georgia. There is also increasing evidence of damaged trees in California's mountain forests (Regens and Rycroft 1988).

Global warming is the result of accumulating carbon dioxide, methane, chlorofluorocarbons (CFCs), ozone, and nitrous oxide in the upper atmosphere. These gases form a filter which allows sunlight to enter, but traps radiant heat, much like a greenhouse. Researchers speculate that this effect has caused a slow rise in the temperature of the surface of the earth, about one degree Fahrenheit over the past century. Global warming is a concern because it may result in a significant shift in weather patterns. Climatological modeling predicts that the earth's middle latitudes will increase at twice the global average. This may result in a temperature increase of half a degree per decade in North America, Europe, and Asia (Corson 1990). While a degree or two may appear insignificant, global temperature averages today are only six to nine degrees warmer than during the Ice Age. Over the past century Atlantic Ocean levels have already risen by one foot in the northeastern United States. The EPA estimates that ocean levels may rise by as much as seven feet by the year 2100 if global warming continues, leaving large portions of densely populated coastal plains underwater (Leatherman 1988). Moreover, forests and crops are sensitive to climate change. A small warming would shift forest zones by as much as 125 miles. Since agriculture is based on regional climate, shifting weather patterns would have long-range implications. As temperatures rise and precipitation decreases, crop yields will decrease. Photosynthesis will accelerate, causing greater competition for nutrients by opportunistic weedy plants (Corson 1990).

Depletion of the ozone layer is equally serious. While in lower altitudes ozone is a main contributor to smog, in upper altitudes ozone functions to filter out ultraviolet radiation. These ultraviolet rays, particularly UV-B, are harmful to people, animals, and certain plants. The ozone layer is created by oxygen molecules which come into contact with ultraviolet radiation. UV radiation splits oxygen molecules (O_2). These oxygen atoms combine with other oxygen atoms to form ozone (O_3). When chemicals such as CFCs, halon, nitrous oxides, carbon dioxide, and methane raise to the upper atmosphere, they disrupt the ozone bonding process. A study done by the Worldwatch Institute (Paper 87, 1988) found that global ozone levels have decreased by 2 percent since 1969, with higher levels of degradation over urban areas of North and South America, Europe, Australia, and New Zealand. Ozone levels dropped by 10 percent over Melbourne, Australia, during December 1987, causing a UV increase of 20 percent (*Washington Post* 1988a; 1989a; 1989b). Exposure to UV radiation may cause sunburn, thickening of the skin, and ultimately thinning of the epidermis. It may also cause non-melanoma skin cancer and malignant melanoma. Eye damage—including cataracts, retinal damage, corneal tumors, and snowblindness—has been tied to UV radiation. Additionally, various cancers, nutritional deficiencies, infectious diseases, and autoimmune disorders are aggravated by UV exposure.

Air pollution is a serious problem in the United States and abroad. Acid rain, global warming, and ozone depletion are worldwide problems. This, in large part, is a consequence of the mobility of airborne pollutants. The result is that high-polluting countries, such as the United States, contribute to significant environmental degradation on a global basis. Thus, in addition to posing a serious threat to public health, airborne pollutants threaten global ecological balance.

The Tension Between Liberalism and Clean Air

Like other areas of environmental quality, liberalism presents a challenge to clean air in two respects. First, the problematic definition of communal good places private rights ahead of communal rights, making clean air legislation subservient to private property claims. Second, capitalism itself fosters air pollution by encouraging expanding production and discouraging conservation.

Air Quality and Communal Good

Reflecting its Lockean Liberal legacy, American political culture places an emphasis on property rights, producing a policy structure which fosters economic growth and "competitiveness." Consequently, clean air policy, like other policy areas, has been subject to an economic litmus test. This was reflected in President Bush's demand that the 1990 Clean Air Act not "harm" the economy. While concepts like "competitiveness" and "not harming the economy" are inherently vague and subjective, they reflect the Lockean commitment to economic self-interest. Communal good has consistently been placed behind property rights in legislative priorities. Even existing regulations are vulnerable. The deadlines in the 1970 Clean Air Act, for example, have been extended four times, allowing compliance to drag well into the next century.

The single largest constraint to clean air is the cost. Implementation of the 1970 Clean Air Act through 1988 was estimated to cost $60 billion, with an additional $80 billion needed to bring the nation into compliance (*New York Times* 1988a). Between 1975 and 1986 public and private expenditures for controlling pollution came to approximately $564 billion, 60 percent of which was paid by the private sector (Department of Commerce 1989:204–5). Policy makers are keenly aware of costs, and thus seek to justify legislation in economic terms. As a consequence, policy efficaciousness is typically evaluated through benefit-cost analyses.

Such analyses are problematic in their purely quantitative approach. While expenditures lend themselves to quantitative analysis, benefits such as improved environmental quality do not. Studies focus, for example, on the costs of implementing control technologies, or the costs for treating diseases directly attributable to environmental toxins, but fail to estimate the broader costs of environmental illness or the qualitative costs of pollution. What is the value of clean air? It is not simply the sum of expenditures saved. Can one quantify aesthetic benefits? And, perhaps most difficult, what is the value of a life saved? In Lave's 1981 study, calculations on the value of a human life varied from an average person's lost future earnings (sixty-three thousand dollars), to a "willingness to pay" criteria, including compensation for pain and suffering ($1.5 million). Such analyses echo Oscar Wilde's comment about those who know "the price of everything and value of nothing" (Beswick 1989).

Furthermore, evaluating objective costs is, in and of itself, a problem, as agencies often differ in estimates. Table 4.1 reviews the estimated costs associated with air pollution controls between 1979 and 1990. The data presented by the Council on Environmental Quality show costs to be approximately 30 percent higher than a similar study done by the Environmental Protection Agency. While expenditure studies are presented as arithmetic fact, the reality is that in deciding which economic indicators to use agencies rely on some discretionary—even ideological—bias.

The main question facing policy makers focuses on how much government, industry, and the public is willing to spend on clean air, and ultimately, who should pay most. The traditional debate has tended to pit environmental quality against jobs. But this misses the point. Relative to GNP, environmental spending is small. The $90 billion American businesses spend annually to comply with environmental legislation comes to about 1.5 percent of GNP (Portney 1990:11). Economists generally agree that environmental compliance has not significantly affected GNP growth, nor has it contributed significantly to a rise in the consumer price index (Rosenbaum 1991:81). In fact, such spending has been a diminishing percentage of new capital investment, from 4.2 percent in 1975 to 1.7 percent in 1987 (Rosenbaum 1991:8; Department of Commerce 1989).

Further, public opinion polls since 1981 suggest that a growing proportion of Americans feel that environmental quality should be pursued regardless of cost. A 1989 *New York Times* and CBS Evening News Poll found that 75 percent of the sample surveyed agreed with the following statement: "Protecting the environment is so important that requirements and standards cannot be too high, and continuing environmental improvements must be made regardless of cost" (Rosenbaum 1991:25–26). Only 19 percent disagreed. Nonetheless, policy makers continue to be reluctant to accept policy proposals that appear to slow economic growth.

The Tension between Capitalism and Clean Air

In order to ease the environmental burden, it is necessary to implement an integrated program of cutting waste, improving energy efficiency, recycling, and cogeneration. Rather than merely retrofiting equipment, American industry must redesign mills and plants to maximize energy use. And, similarly, consumers must rethink their reliance on consumer goods with short usable life-spans. This, however, would create a short-term economic decline as industry and consumers absorbed the costs of new technologies. Moreover, American capitalism is based on a con-

TABLE 4.1. Comparative Estimates of Air Pollution Control Costs

Council on Environmental Quality Estimate for 1979, and for 1979–1988 (billions of 1984 dollars)

Sector	Annual Cost 1979	Projected Cumulative Costs 1979–1988
Governments	$ 2.15	$ 27.89
Industrial	6.26	84.08
Electric Utilities	12.02	150.15
Mobile Sources	11.59	165.59
Total	32.02	427.71

Source: Table 3.8 in Portney 1990:65.

Adapted from Council on Environmental Quality, *Environmental Quality: 1980* (Washington, D.C.: GPO, 1980), 394.

Environmental Protection Agency Estimate for 1981 and for 1981–1990 (billions of 1984 dollars)

Sector	Annual Cost 1981	Projected Cumulative Costs 1981–1990
Government[a]	$ 0.72	$ 6.29
Industrial[b]	7.21	84.67
Electric Utilities	8.49	109.08
Mobile Sources	6.90	91.83
Total	23.32	291.87

[a]The sum of government expenditures and municipal waste incineration entries in the EPA report.

[b]All entries other than electric utilities, mobile sources, and government and municipal waste incineration.

Source: Table 3.9 in Portney (1990:66). Adapted from Office of Policy Analysis, Environmental Protection Agency, "The Cost of Clean Air and Water Report to Congress, 1984," Report no. EPA-230-05-84-008 (May 1984) 11–12.

sumption ethic that encourages waste. Extending the usable life of consumer goods necessarily affects industrial productivity. If consumers really reused and conserved consumer products, demand for manufactured goods would drop and economic growth would slow.

One of the best examples of the conflict between capitalism and clean air was the dismantling of urban transit systems by General Motors. GM's actions are illustrative because they expose the limited foresight capability of Liberal society and the impact of self-interested corporations seeking to maximize profits. In 1936, General Motors, along with Greyhound, Standard Oil of California, and Firestone Rubber, established National City Lines (NCL) as a holding company with the intent of buying local transit companies and replacing electric railcars and buses with diesel buses—buses built by GM, with tires by Firestone, operated by Greyhound, and fueled by Standard Oil.

After taking over several transit companies in the northeast, NCL established Pacific City Lines as a West Coast subsidiary. By 1940, PCL was looking toward the vast rail system in southern California, Pacific Electric's red cars. Constructed in 1911, the red car system stretched to all cities within a seventy-five-mile radius of Los Angeles. After acquiring Pacific Electric, PCL dismantled the tracks in downtown Los Angeles, the nucleus of the system, replacing them with loud, smoky buses. This had two immediate effects. First, it made it impossible to utilize fully the remaining tracks. And, it made travel by mass transit an uncomfortable, cumbersome experience. Ultimately, it left the private automobile as the only reliable transportation (Snell 1985).

In the end, the company bought and dismantled over one hundred electric transit systems in cities from sixteen states, including New York, Philadelphia, Baltimore, St. Louis, Oakland, Salt Lake City, and, of course, Los Angeles. The American reliance on private cars came as a direct result of GM's actions. The impact on air quality is clear; vehicle traffic alone accounts for 36 percent of airborne pollutants (EPA 1989a). By 1973, when urban mass transit again became a local issue, Los Angeles estimated it would cost $6.6 billion for a system one-sixth the size of the original Pacific Electric system (Snell 1985).

The inability of Liberal society to anticipate the negative impact private corporate action may take on the community, and the reluctance of Liberal society to prohibit such actions, causes a direct conflict between liberalism and communal good—in this case a conflict between liberalism and clean air. Any legislative proposal that inhibits economic freedom is quickly attacked. Early drafts of the 1990 Clean Air Act (HR 3054 and HR 2666) were criticized for their strict standards and deadlines, and its consequent costs:

> HR 3054 uses a shotgun approach, hitting a wide range of emissions control targets. This at best might bring a few areas into attainment a few years earlier [but] could trigger economic downturns in many areas . . . we are opposed to . . . a fee on the sales of gasoline and diesel fuel in areas classified as severe health endangerment areas . . . it would force consumers and the petroleum industry to bear the burden of a problem which . . . is often overstated and poorly understood. (William O'Keefe, vice-president

of the American Petroleum Institute, testifying at the House
Committee on Energy and Commerce, 9/28/87)

This point is made repeatedly by political action committees representing industries opposed to strict clean air legislation. As if to reinforce
the point, these PACs distributed $28,312,111 to congressional incum-
bents between June 1981 and April 1990. Of this, PACs representing
General Motors, Ford, and Chrysler, along with the National Automobile Dealers Association, gave $6.4 million (Associated Press 1990).

Corporate opposition to strong anti–air-pollution regulations has
consistently focused on economic costs. William O'Keefe, vice-president
and chief operating officer of the American Petroleum Institute, argued
that policy makers must keep in mind other goals of the American people when considering clean air legislation, specifically "the expansion of
economic growth and opportunity" (Environmental Protection Subcommittee of the Senate Environment and Public Works Committee
Hearing, Sept. 21, 1989). In arguing against the Clean Air Act, Samuel
Leonard, director of Automotive Emission Control at General Motors,
warned of "causing undue disruption [to] the Nation's economy" (Senate Environmental Protection Subcommittee, Sept. 28, 1989). Richard
Lawson, president of the National Coal Association, similarly argued
that "environmental goals must be founded on sound science and . . .
must be reasonably balanced with the equally important goals of energy
security and economic growth" (Senate Environmental Protection Committee, Oct. 3, 1989).

In balancing corporate interests with clean air, policy makers have
consistently diluted legislation to accommodate economic growth. The
dilemma for policy makers is how to satisfy public demand for cleaner
air while maintaining a fundamental commitment to economic expansion. The following section explores the evolution of clean air legislation, with a concern to the symbolic policies that helped ease the tension
between economics and clean air.

Symbolic Politics in Clean Air Legislation

Clean air policy since 1970 has explicitly sought to satisfy public demand, while deadline extensions and bureaucratic obstacles have kept
legislation from being fully implemented. Further, clean air legislation
has consistently been marketed deceptively. This section explores the
evolution of clean air policy, focusing on the symbolic aspects of the
1970 and 1990 Clean Air Acts.

Air Policy Through 1970

Initial air policy focused only on research to identify the extent of pollution dangers. Contemporary air policy at the federal level began with the Air Pollution Control Act in 1955, which provided funding for research grants and granted federal research authority. The 1963 Clean Air Act provided federal grants to states and local programs aimed at encouraging improvement; it also created a conference procedure for interstate air pollution. The 1967 Air Quality Act created deadlines for states to create air quality standards; it also allowed for the Department of Health, Education, and Welfare (then HEW) to set those standards if states failed to do so, but no action was taken. Economic pressures at the local and state level are often too strong for the adoption of tough laws, making federal intervention necessary. Kenski and Ingram (1986) describe early policies as noncoercive and nonregulatory. They point out that it was the failure of these "noninterventionist" policies that ultimately led to the evolution of stronger policy.

The 1970 Clean Air Act

Following the mobilization of mass public demand for strong environmental regulation a different dynamic emerged. With urban air pollution at an all-time high, it became clear that the traditional noninterventionist models of policy were inadequate. Following Earth Day, the 1970 Clean Air Act (PL 91–604) was enacted. Jones (1974) argues that the 1970 act was a public-satisfying policy response:

> Public officials are sensitive to large scale public expression on issues. Normally, of course, the message from the general public on issues is ambiguous: some vaguely for, some vaguely against, most indifferent . . . However general were the instructions on E-Day, there was an unambiguous call for action . . . it seems possible that a congressional majority was prepared to enact strong legislation in 1970. (Jones 1974)

The act established the most stringent pollution controls to date, relying on states to enforce compliance. It created 247 air quality control regions across the United States that were to meet National Ambient Air Quality Standards (NAAQS) set by federal guidelines. The NAAQS would be set by the EPA, establishing pollutant levels acceptable to protect human health and environmental conditions. The act established primary standards intended to protect the health of the most vulnerable populations, including infants and the elderly. All regions were to meet the

NAAQS by 1982. Secondary standards were established to protect crops, water, and buildings, with no compliance deadline. The NAAQS were significant because the act required that they be established according to a human health criterion, without regard to cost.

The responsibility for implementing the act fell upon the states, each of which was required to develop and submit for EPA approval a State Implementation Plan (SIP) outlining how it would enforce the federal guidelines. These guidelines included specific requirements for stationary sources. In problem regions, factories were required to retrofit equipment with pollution controls. In particularly poor regions, factories were required to retrofit with controls representing the "best available technology." New factories were required to "offset" their emissions by paying existing factories to reduce emissions or by supplying these factories with control equipment. As well, the EPA was to establish new source-performance standards (NSPS) according to industry. Mobile source (vehicle) emissions were similarly strong. New cars were required to meet standards that would reduce hydrocarbon and carbon monoxide emissions by 90 percent by 1975. Nitrogen oxide emissions were required to meet a 90 percent reduction by 1976.

What is immediately apparent in the 1970 act are the stringent standards and ambitious goals. Considering the quality of air in 1970, mandating that all air quality regions meet the same primary requirements within twelve years suggests some wishful thinking. Mandating a 90 percent reduction in hydrocarbon and carbon monoxide emissions within five years suggests that the framers of the act assumed that standards would not be met. What then is the act attempting? Jones (1974) considers the Clean Air Act an example of speculative public policy. The act is sufficiently bold so as to preclude any realistic expectation of meeting the standards. The thought behind this, Jones argues, is that industry will push to reach its highest potential if not the actual standards.

What evolved, however, was an environment of assumed noncompliance by large sectors of industry. It was cheaper, in many cases, to pay fines rather than install the equipment necessary to meet the standards. The enforcement mechanisms of the act are, to a large extent, at the root of noncompliance. While penalties included fines of up to twenty-five thousand dollars per day of violation and up to one year in jail, the stringency of the punitive measures is misleading. Section 112 of the act instructs the EPA administrator to regulate stationary sources when such pollutants may "cause or contribute to any increase in mortality or an increase in serious irreversible or incapacitating illness." The language allows the administrator significant discretion in applying sanctions (Rosenbaum 1985:118).

Ten years into the act high levels of noncompliance remained. By 1980 the percentage of major stationary sources out of compliance were as follows: integrated iron and steel plants, 87 percent; other iron and steel plants, 29 percent; primary smelters, 54 percent; pulp and paper manufacturers, 13 percent; municipal incinerators, 17 percent; petroleum refineries, 21 percent; aluminum reduction, 24 percent; portland cement factories, 12 percent; and power plants, 20 percent (CEQ 1980). Similarly, most major cities were out of compliance at least several days per year. As Table 4.2 outlines, some cities were out of compliance as much as one out of every three days during the 1980s, and Los Angeles was out of compliance nearly two out of three days. By 1985 fewer than 60 percent of the states had even approved SIPs, effectively preventing enforcement (Rosenbaum 1985:110).

While the deadlines of the act are explicit, administrators have used their discretionary authority to extend them. The act allowed extensions when, in the opinion of the EPA administrator, compliance would impose a severe or unequal hardship. Again, such a determination is up to the discretion of the administrator. Rosenbaum (1985) argues that the protracted administrative process necessary to impose punitive measures often forces regulators to seek voluntary compliance:

> [Regulators] want to avoid penalties as a means of ensuring compliance if possible because they know that resorting to administrative or judicial tribunals likely will involve a protracted, inflexible process with no assurances that the polluter will be compelled to control emissions speedily and efficiently at the conclusion. In fact, polluters often provoke such action, hoping to avoid emission controls indefinitely by exploiting the complexities of the administrative or judicial procedures involved. (Rosenbaum 1985:122)

The long history of the act's continual extensions illustrates the point. In 1973 the EPA granted a one-year extension of auto emission deadlines in response to the Arab oil embargo. The Energy Supply and Environmental Coordination Act of 1974 provided waivers to certain Clean Air Act requirements in an effort to increase the use of coal. By 1977, in the face of new economic and energy concerns, Congress extended all emission deadlines for two more years. The deadlines were to be followed by tighter hydrocarbon and nitrogen oxide standards (Clean Air Act amendments of 1977—PL 95–95). The Carter administration was able to push forward minimal advances. The Toxic Substances Control Act in 1978, for example, mandated the elimination of all but essential uses of chloroflourocarbons (CFCs) as an aerosol propellant. In

TABLE 4.2. Air Quality Trends in Major Urban Areas 1980–1990

Number of PSI[1] days greater than 100

PMSA[2]	1980	1981	1982	1983	1984	1985	1986	1987	1988	1989	1990
Atlanta	7	9	5	23	8	9	17	19	15	3	16
Boston	8	2	5	16	6	2	0	5	11	1	1
Chicago	na	3	31	14	8	4	5	9	18	2	3
Dallas	10	12	11	17	10	12	5	6	3	3	5
Denver	35	51	52	67	59	37	43	34	18	11	7
Detroit	na	18	19	18	7	2	6	9	17	12	3
Houston	10	32	25	43	30	30	28	31	31	19	35
Kansas City	13	7	0	4	12	4	8	5	3	2	2
Los Angeles	220	228	195	184	208	196	210	187	226	212	163
New York	119	100	69	65	53	21	16	16	35	9	10
Philadelphia	52	29	44	56	31	25	21	36	34	19	11
Pittsburgh	20	17	14	36	24	6	9	15	31	11	12
San Francisco	2	1	2	4	2	5	4	1	1	0	1
Seattle	33	42	19	19	4	26	18	13	8	4	2
Washington	38	23	25	53	30	15	11	23	34	7	5

[1]Pollutant Standard Index

[2]Primary Metropolitan Statistical Area

na = not available

NAAQS primary standards were aimed at protecting human health with an adequate margin of safety for all segments of the population, including infants and the elderly. The PSI (Pollution Standard Index) is an aggregate index of the concentrations of five of the six major air pollutants (Particulate Matter [TSP], Sulfer Oxides, Nitrogen Oxides, Volatile Organic Compounds, Carbon Monoxide. Lead was measured as a constituent of TSP.) The days above a healthful level are also above NAAQS aggregate levels.

Source: U.S. EPA, Office of Air Quality Planning and Standards, National Air Quality and Emissions Trends Report, 1990, EPA-450/4-91-023 (Research Triangle Park, NC: EPA, November 1991).

1979 Carter established several programs aimed at controlling acid rain, including the establishment of the Acid Rain Coordination Committee. Finally, in 1980, the Acid Precipitation Act created the National Acid Precipitation Assessment Program (NAPAP) authorizing research only.

Reagan's election put a halt to Carter's progress. Reagan's appointment of Anne (Gorsuch) Burford as EPA administrator seriously undercut all previous environmental achievements. By 1983 Reagan's anti-environmentalism softened in the face of public criticism, and Burford was replaced by Ruckelshaus. After six years of anti-environmental action, Reagan, in a symbolic gesture, signed the instrument of final ratification of the Convention for the Protection of the Ozone Layer. In 1987 new clean air amendments were introduced in both the House and the Senate. However, the One Hundredth Congress adjourned before any significant action was taken. By 1989 George Bush proposed a new Clean Air Act, aimed at cleaning up the nation's air without "harming" the economy.

Overall, emissions have improved slightly since 1970. The significant reduction of particulate matter and lead emissions accounts for most air quality improvement (see Table 4.3). Yet most urban areas have failed to attain ambient air quality standards, and in many areas ozone levels have risen significantly. The 1988 ozone composite average was less than 1 percent lower than 1983, which was the highest composite average during the ten-year period from 1979 to 1988 (EPA 1990).

Emissions of sulfur oxides, nitrogen oxides, volatile organic compounds, and carbon monoxide have not been significantly reduced as a result of the 1970 Clean Air Act or its 1977 amendments. As a consequence, there has been increasing demand for renewed commitment on the part of government in addressing air quality.

The 1990 Clean Air Act

The 1990 Clean Air Act amendments ended a decade of legislative gridlock on air policy. Throughout the 1980s attempts to pass Clean Air legislation were consistently beaten by a hostile administration and a coalition of utilities, automotive manufacturers, oil companies, labor unions, and midwestern congressional representatives who feared greater regulation of the auto industry and utilities in the Ohio Valley. By the late 1980s this coalition began to fracture as public concern for increased environmental action rose and as midwestern interests came into conflict with the interests of other regions of the country (Smith 1992).

TABLE 4.3. Nationwide Emission Estimates 1940–1990 (in million metric tons)

Pollutant	1940	1950	1960	1970	1980	1985	1990
PM/TSP	23.1	24.9	21.6	18.5	8.5	7.2	7.5
SO_2	17.6	19.8	19.7	28.3	23.4	21.1	21.2
NO_2	6.8	9.3	12.8	18.3	20.4	19.9	19.6
VOC	18.1	20.2	22.6	26.2	21.1	20.1	18.7
CO	81.5	86.1	88.1	100.2	77.0	68.7	60.1
(Pb)(ggms)	na	na	na	203.8	70.6	20.1	7.1

ggms (gigagrams) = 1,000 metric tons
na = not available
PM/ TSP = Particulate Matter/Total Suspended Particulates
SO_2 = Sulfer Dioxide
NO_2 = Nitrogen Dioxide
VOC = Volatile Organic Compounds
CO = Carbon Monoxide
Pb = Lead

Sources: Environmental Protection Agency, 1989, *National Air Pollutant Emission Estimates, 1940–1987* (March), table 1; Environmental Protection Agency, 1990, *National Air Quality and Emissions Trends Report, 1988* (March), tables 3.1, 3.2, 3.3, 3.4, 3.5, 3.6.

The 1990 amendments address several issues the 1970 act ignored. The 1990 amendments address ozone based smog, acid rain, CFCs, and air toxins. In ozone nonattainment areas, specific pollution controls are mandated for all stationary sources, from industry to bakeries to gasoline stations, based on the variable deadlines below (Title 1). In the serious ozone nonattainment areas reformulated petroleum fuels are mandated for mobile sources to reduce ozone-causing VOCs (Title 2). In an effort to reduce mobile source emissions further the act requires the EPA administrator to issue regulations requiring commercial fleets (excluding emergency vehicles) of ten or more capable of being centrally fueled to use "clean fuels"—such as methanol, ethanol, propane, and natural gas. Additionally, the administrator must develop particulate matter standards for urban buses and PM emissions must reach a level 50 percent lower than that of conventional heavy duty vehicles by model year 1994. To initiate similar technology for private vehicles, the act authorizes a pilot program to be implemented in California. The program calls for 150,000 clean fuel vehicles in each model year starting 1996, growing to 300,000 by 1999 (Title 2).

Further, the act identifies by name 189 chemicals determined to be hazardous to human health. Industries must cut emissions of these air toxins to a level equal to the average of the twelve cleanest similar facilities. If, by 2003, facilities still pose a cancer danger to one person in ten thousand after using the best available technology, the firm will be shut down. Extensions to 2020 may be granted to steel industry coke ovens if interim conditions are met (Title 3).

The new amendments cover two other shortcomings of the original act. Forty million dollars were set aside for five years of research into pollutants that reduce visibility, particularly in the national parks. In addition, the amendments establish $250 million dollars over five years to help those workers displaced by the act who have enrolled in job-retraining programs (Title 11).

On the whole the 1990 Clean Air Act offers significant improvements to previous air policies. However, the act falls short in several ways. Regional deadlines for meeting the national ambient air quality standards (NAAQS) established in the 1970 act were extended for up to twenty years, depending on the area: "marginal" areas must meet the ozone standard by 1993 (thirty-nine cities); "moderate" areas have until 1996 (thirty-two cities); "serious" areas until 1999 (sixteen cities); "severe" areas until 2005–7 (eight cities); and one "extreme" area (Los Angeles) until 2010 (PL 101–549, Title 1).

The continued reliance on fossil fuels—specifically coal-burning power plants and petroleum-based industries—betrays a commitment to short-term economic growth at the expense of long-term clean air potential. While the various controls outlined above will encourage cleaner usage of fossil fuels, they fail to encourage the exploration of alternative energy technologies—technologies that increase efficiency, lower emissions, and are renewable.

Alternative energy sources such as geothermal utilities, alcohol vehicle fuels, and waste to energy facilities are already operating on a small scale. The electricity generated by geothermal sources worldwide was estimated to reach 6,400 megawatts in 1990, equaling the output of six large nuclear power plants (WRI & IIED 1989; National Research Council 1987). Alcohol-based fuels, including ethanol (ethyl alcohol), methanol (ethanol and methane), and gasohol (gasoline and ethanol), offer renewable fuels that burn cleaner than conventional gasoline and diesel. Ethanol, produced from any number of crops—including sugarcane, corn, wood, and organic solid waste—has a high oxygen content, allowing more efficient combustion. Alcohol-burning vehicles emit little or no nitrogen oxides or hydrocarbons, reducing ozone smog. Organic wastes, including biodegradable solid waste, animal waste, plants, and even garbage, can be processed to produce methane, a renewable natural gas. And facilities using cogeneration allow waste steam from industry to heat surrounding areas and provide local electrical generation.

While these technologies would provide substantial improvements in air quality, they are expensive, and they challenge the economic hegemony of petroleum corporations within the energy industry. Oil is relatively cheap, especially considering the subsidies provided by the U.S. Department of Energy and the armed forces. Federal funding of fossil fuel energy research in 1990 was five times greater than research for renewable energy sources, approximately $650 million to $132 million (Holdren 1991). Further, the Defense Department subsidizes the oil industry by ensuring access to overseas petroleum. The Gulf War was clearly fought to secure oil reserves in Kuwait, Saudi Arabia, and the United Arab Emirates, at a cost of over $100 billion (Mandel 1991).

Moreover, by relying on traditional models of EPA administrator discretion, the act allows the public health criteria for air quality enforcement to remain vulnerable to the political criteria of the current administration. This was clearly illustrated during the Reagan years. Since the existing models of voluntary compliance have clearly failed, rigorous and consistent enforcement is necessary to ensure compliance. This is only possible through an increase in the size of the EPA staff.

The mainstream environmental community has been especially critical of the plan. The Sierra Club, National Audobon Society, and the Union of Concerned Scientists have all voiced concerns about what the act fails to do. The air standards for sulfur oxides and air toxins are at significantly weaker levels than those sought by environmentalists, and the deadlines are much farther off. Creative programs, such as urban forestation programs would offer a fundamentally different character to the current legislation. Trees offer two important areas of clean air potential. First, trees absorb CO_2 and release oxygen. Every new tree planted absorbs enough CO_2 to offset the CO_2 emitted from twenty-six thousand average vehicle miles (Comp 1989). In addition, the shade given by trees cools surrounding buildings, reducing the amount of energy needed for air conditioning.

The 1990 amendments are significantly weaker than legislation proposed back in 1987. HR 3054, (Clean Air Amendments, 1987—dead legislation) called for NAAQS deadlines of three years for "moderate areas," five years for "serious areas," and ten years for "severe areas." It would have established a per ton fee on emissions from specific stationary sources in "severe areas." HR 3054 sought a four legged plan to reduce mobile source emissions. It mandated a set percentage of new vehicles nationwide capable of using low-emission fuel, increasing with each model year. It would have prohibited the awarding of federal highway funds to those areas not in compliance with State Implementation Plans. It would have authorized diesel fuel sales fees in "severe areas" which in turn would have provided grant money to local and state governments for ozone and CO_2 control measures. Finally, it would have banned immediately the sale of leaded gasoline. HR 2666 (the Acid Deposition Control Act, 1987—dead) sought to reduce acid rain through enforced SO_2 reductions by 1993. To offset utility-rate increases the plan would have established the Acid Deposition Control Fund to make subsidies available to utilities in compliance. Additionally, the fund would have provided grants to stationary sources to promote new emission control technologies.

Rather than confront the serious impact of a petroleum-based industrial economy, the current air policies simply aim at reducing emissions in technologies that are inherently dirty. By failing to address conservation and alternative fuels seriously, the 1990 amendments fail to offer a true air-quality alternative.

California: Leaving the Federal Model

Like many other jurisdictions, California was slow to comply with the 1970 Clean Air Act amendments. California's State Implementation Plan (SIP), accepted by the EPA under the Reagan administration, argued that southern California simply could not meet federal standards. But, ironically, it was this weak SIP that initiated California's evolution as the leader in innovative clean air policy. The acceptance of California's SIP allowed environmentalists to challenge the EPA's weak implementation of the Clean Air Act in court.

In 1987, after discussions with EPA broke down, the Ninth Circuit Court of Appeals in San Francisco ordered the EPA to reject California's 1984 SIP. Facing potential sanctions, including the loss of federal highway and sewer funds, and with prodding from Rep. Henry Waxman (D-Los Angeles), the California Air Resources Board (CARB), the Air Quality Management District (AQMD), and the Southern California Association of Governments (SCAG) created the Air Quality Management Plan (AQMP) for southern California (Kraft 1993).

California has the nation's worst record for air quality. This, in part, explains why California state air quality officials voted to leave the federal air quality model and institute a stringent twenty-year plan to reduce smog. The plan mandates specific controls to be in place by 2010. The first part of the plan includes 123 immediate controls to be implemented between now and the year 2000. These controls focus on immediate changes based on current technologies, such as reformulating commercial and household paints and solvents to reduce hydrocarbon emissions, regulating charcoal broilers in restaurants, requiring emission control equipment for bakeries and dry cleaners, and more effective inspection of motor vehicles. In addition, the AQMP requires large employers—those employing one hundred people or more—to provide employees with incentives for car pooling and public transit use (Kamienieki and Ferrall 1991).

The second section of the plan depends on the development of new technologies and requires implementation over a fifteen-year period. This portion of the plan mandates that 40 percent of private vehicles and 70 percent of commercial trucks and buses be required to run on nonpetroleum fuels, such as methanol, by 1999. Two percent of all cars sold in 1998, and 10 percent in 2003, must meet zero emission standards. With available technology, only electric vehicles are able to meet that standard. The plan also includes the construction of housing hubs closer to job centers and improved mass transit and car pooling.

The final portion of the plan requires the further evolution of new technologies and therefore focuses on research and development and includes the establishment of an Office of Technology Assessment. The specific controls in this section of the plan include the conversion of motor vehicles to "extremely low-emitting" engines, which may preclude the use of the internal combustion engine (Kraft 1993).

The Air Quality Management Plan is a significant departure from traditional clean air policy models. And, like any innovative plan, it is not problem free. As with the 1970 federal Clean Air Act amendments, industry—particularly automotive and petrochemical companies—has consistently argued that the AQMP presents an unreasonable intrusion of government and that the emission standards are unattainable.

In addition, the plan fails to address population growth and urban development—the most significant roots of southern California's air problem. By the plan's implementation deadline of 2010, southern California's population is expected to grow by 37 percent—from 11.3 million to nearly 15.5 million (SCAQMD 1989). The expected improvement in stationary and mobile emissions will be offset to some degree by an increase in total vehicle mileage and industrial growth. Furthermore, because the AQMP depends on new technologies that are yet to be fully developed, the expected success of the plan may be somewhat optimistic (Kamieniecki and Ferrall 1991).

Nonetheless, the commitment of California to lower emissions through a four-point plan of conservation, alternative fuels, mass transit, and a shift in residential, economic, and social patterns, makes the plan the strongest clean air program in the world. The continued reliance on petroleum-based fuels, private transit, and resistance to conservation make the federal model weak by comparison. It is possible that those regions suffering through critical air quality problems may have to follow California's lead in leaving the federal model in order to achieve significant improvement in air quality.

Accommodating Liberalism: The Hidden Agenda

The 1990 Clean Air Act amendments include an important set of regulations, but the Bush administration's claim of entering a "new era" of air quality is largely symbolic. The Bush administration agenda may be better understood when considering the Presidential Council on Competitiveness, within the OMB. In its first regulatory decision the council, chaired by Quayle, directed EPA administrator William Reilly to cancel the agency's proposed recycling program, arguing that such a program would pose an undue economic burden on the owners of municipal incinerators (*Washington Post* 1990). Recycling is a basic step to improving air quality, but even the minimal investment required to implement such a program seemed to present too much of a challenge to economic growth.

Bush's energy strategy explicitly illustrates the point. Rather than conserve, the proposal focused on increased energy production. Bush sought to open the Arctic National Wildlife Refuge to oil drilling, he pursued greater reliance on nuclear energy, and he favored deregulating electric utilities. Several proposals to conserve energy use were eliminated by the OMB, including efficiency standards for electric lights, tax credits for electricity generated by alternative fuels, loans for efficiency programs, and greater vehicle mileage efficiency standards (Lippman 1991).

Bush used the popularity of environmental protection to cultivate political capital. In the 1988 campaign he took advantage of the high saliency of air quality, marketing himself as an "environmental" president: "I would be a Republican in the Teddy Roosevelt tradition. A conservationist. An Environmentalist" (Bush on the campaign trail, 1988, in Vig and Kraft, 1990c). Yet his social, economic, and political networks betray his relationship to high emission industries. Bush made his fortune as a Texas oil man, founding several petroleum companies, including Bush-Overby, Zapata Petroleum, and Zapata Offshore Oil (Dye 1986).

Because of the highly complex technologies involved in environmental improvement, Bush was able to present the 1990 Clean Air Act as a promise to clear the air, while in fact reinforcing a commitment to business as usual. The Bush record, while better than Reagan's, represents a fundamental commitment to economic growth, with only secondary regard for long-term air quality.

Both the 1970 and the 1990 Clean Air Act amendments were passed by conservative administrations seeking to satisfy public demand for strong air policy in an effort to ease discontent in an increasingly difficult arena of public policy, while maintaining a commitment to economic growth. While the acts were written fairly strictly, the specific language allows weak action through discretionary extensions of deadlines and lax enforcement.

The 1990 amendments extend, once again, the original 1970 deadlines. While the air quality standards of the act will improve air quality to some extent, the continual extensions of deadlines and the weak enforcement mechanisms remain problematic. The climate of continual extensions has given industry the impression that standards may again be extended, removing any incentive of voluntary compliance. The noncompliance we have seen in the past can be expected to continue; and so, the poor air quality we are now experiencing can be expected to continue, with minimal improvements.

What is more telling, perhaps, is what was left out of the new amendments. In following the model established in 1970, the 1990 amendments fail to address the core problems of air pollution: petroleum-based technologies and wasteful consumption. Rather than initiate alternative technologies the amendments attempt to clean up old technologies. If clean air was truly the central concern of the act, the plan would mandate conservation, cogeneration, and recycling, as well as an increase in mass transit funds and alternative energy research grants. It would also establish safer air standards and emission limits. Without dealing with the issue of waste and petroleum-based technologies, the same air problems will exist twenty years from now, and Congress will be debating the 2010 Clean Air Act.

The Clinton-Gore approach to the environmental arena is significantly different than those of either Reagan or Bush. During the 1992 campaign Clinton outlined an ambitious environmental policy approach. The plan includes four strategies:

1. reducing solid and hazardous waste through conservation and expanded recycling markets;
2. preserving wetland and wilderness areas;
3. creating economic incentives for maintaining environmental quality; and

4. exerting American leadership for improving global environmental quality. (Clinton and Gore 1992).

Clinton's appointment of Browner to head the EPA and Babbitt to run Interior suggests a substantively different approach than that of Reagan or Bush. But the Clinton strategy remains with the Liberal tradition. Clinton, like Gore (1992), insists that environmental quality can be improved using market incentives, such as marketing pollution rights.

The 1990 Clean Air Act, the Air Quality Management Plan (AQMP) for southern California, and the Clinton environmental approach all rely heavily on market mechanisms. Market incentives rely on economic self-interest to motivate regulated parties to comply with federal and state standards. By giving industry the opportunity to buy or bank "pollution rights," market incentives are thought to give regulated parties greater flexibility and control. This flexibility is thought to motivate a higher level of compliance (Cohen and Kamieniecki 1991).

Such mechanisms, however, do not ease the tensions between liberalism and environmental quality. Rather, such mechanisms appease the tension. Specifically, there are two concerns with the market approach. First, it continues to place individual self-interest above any substantive notion of community interest. Second, with the low level of compliance in previous policy models, there is little reason to assume that market models will engender any greater compliance. The basis of market incentives is to punish polluters and reward environmentally friendly—"green"—business practices. The rationale is only valid when compliance coincides with self-interest. What happens when self-interest dictates noncompliance? To date there is little evidence to show that market mechanisms are any more effective than command and control mechanisms.

Clinton and Gore, as unabashed environmentalists, offer hope but little substance. Within days of taking office the Clinton administration declared that the deficit was more severe than anticipated and consequently Americans were going to have to wait for the Clinton proposals to become policy. For Reagan, Bush, and Clinton, economic growth has remained the central priority.

Conclusion

This chapter has argued that the tension between liberalism and clean air has been eased through symbolic policies. Liberalism's narrow self-interest model is inconsistent with clean air in two respects. On the one hand, the limited notion of communal good places private rights ahead of communal rights. On the other, capitalism has traditionally encouraged air pollution by relying on continual growth and economic expansion. Clean air policy since 1970 has been explicitly public satisfying, while bureaucratic posturing has precluded full implementation of clean air regulations. Also, clean air legislation has been marketed deceptively. Bush held up the 1990 act as heralding a "new era for clean air," when in fact the Act is simply a weaker version of the 1970 Clean Air act. The acts sought to satisfy public demand for strong clean air policy while maintaining a commitment to traditional Liberal concerns of economic growth.

The following chapters continue the analysis in the substantive areas of water, waste, and energy. Ultimately, the study explores the choices Liberal society must confront in dealing with increasing environmental degradation.

5   Water Policy

In a typical year almost 449 trillion gallons of rain falls in the United States, enough to supply each American with six thousand gallons every day (Rosenbaum 1985). Ninety percent of that water is consumed by industry and agriculture. The entire industrial economy is based on the abundance of clean water. And, though there clearly is a limit to the availability of water, the United States continues to consume more water per capita than any other nation (see Table 5.1). As Table 5.2 illustrates, water consumption has increased dramatically since World War II, both as a result of an increasing population and of the rapid expansion of industry.

Rather than viewing water as a resource used in common, Liberal society views water as property regulated by the market. As a result, water is developed and used according to private needs—with little regard for communal need. Furthermore, capitalism has encouraged the degradation of water quality. As private property, water has been viewed as a raw resource to be exploited for profit. The characterization of water as an economic commodity carries serious implications. Most important, it suggests that water users have little or no responsibility to assure that water, once used, maintains its value. Thus, upstream polluters have historically refused any demand to clean up waste water. Rivers and streams have been diverted, runoff has introduced toxic metals and phosphates into groundwater, and industrial waste has destroyed lakes and estuaries. Deteriorating water quality is a direct result of the economic origins of water development and use.

This chapter explores the tension between liberalism and the development of water resources. The chapter then argues that water policy, like air policy, seeks to accommodate that tension through regulation which appears strong but is in reality a tiger without teeth. In this sense water policy is largely symbolic. The chapter begins by evaluating the content and consequences of water pollution. It then explores the development and use of water resources from the perspective of Lasswell's (1938) "who gets what, when, and how," examining

TABLE 5.1. Estimated Water Withdrawals by Country, 1980

Country	Total (billion liters per day)	Per Capita (thousand liters per day)
United States	1,683	7.2
Canada	120	4.8
Soviet Union	967	3.6
Japan	306	2.6
Mexico	149	2.0
India	1,058	1.5
United Kingdom	78	1.4
Poland	46	1.3
China	1,260	1.2
Indonesia	115	0.7

Source: Sandra Postel, *Water: Rethinking Management in an Age of Scarcity*, Worldwatch Paper 62 (Washington, DC: Worldwatch Institute, December 1984).

TABLE 5.2 U.S. Water Withdrawals per Day, 1940–1985

Year	Billion Gallons
1940	140
1950	180
1960	270
1970	370
1980	450
1985	400

Source: U.S. Bureau of the Census, *Statistical Abstract of the United States: 1988* (Washington, DC: 1987), 191.

the shift in the philosophy of water usage: from traditional riparian water rights, requiring that any water diverted from its stream be returned in the same condition, to economic water rights, defining water as an economic commodity. Ultimately, the chapter explores the specific symbolic elements of water policy.

Background: The Content and Consequences of Water Pollution

Water quality is degraded through a variety of pollution sources. As sewer systems continue to age and deteriorate, growing populations produce increasing demands. The result is the seepage of raw sewage into aquifers. Improper discharge from millions of septic tanks exacerbates the problem, making sewage the single largest polluter of drinking water. As well, waste disposal sites pose special dangers. There are currently about 180,000 pits, ponds, and lagoons each leaching waste into groundwater. Nearly 29,000 hazardous waste sites have been identified as potential candidates for Superfund. As many as 500 hazardous waste land sites and 16,000 landfills present potential leaching of hazardous waste into water (Rosenbaum 1991).

Agriculture sprays millions of tons of fertilizers and pesticides on crops, which ultimately seep into water sources. Runoff from fields, feedlots, and barnyards carries potassium and nitrogen into ground and surface waters. Water diverted from rivers for irrigation is returned with excessive levels of salt and minerals, degrading drinking-water sources. For example, during dry periods the Red River running through Oklahoma and Texas often becomes saltier than seawater (Corson 1990). Similarly, Colorado River water becomes increasingly sodium rich as it makes its way south, causing serious problems for communities such as Los Angeles which rely heavily on the Colorado for drinking water (Rosenbaum 1991). Sodium finds its way into water in more direct ways as well. Road salt used to de-ice roads in the East and the Midwest increase chloride concentrations in groundwater by as much as ten times (Rosenbaum 1985).

Mine runoff brings high levels of acid, iron, sulfates, copper, lead, uranium, and other hazardous materials into aquifers and pollutes as many as twelve thousand miles of streams in the United States (Rosenbaum 1985; Corson 1990). Sulfur and nitrogen oxides released into the air cause acid precipitation, increasing the acidity of aquifers, lakes, streams, and rivers. In Chesapeake Bay and other waters of the Northeast, acid is a central pollutant. The increased acidity caused by mining and acid rain kills aquatic life and poisons water by dissolving the toxic metals in the surrounding soil (aluminum, cadmium, and mercury) and copper and lead in water pipes (Corson 1990). This problem will only grow worse with the increasing reliance on coal.

More than 80 percent of community water systems rely on groundwater, making groundwater contamination one of the most serious public health hazards (Rosenbaum 1991). As Table 5.3 illustrates, sewage, underground storage tanks, agriculture, landfills, and abandoned waste sites remain major sources of groundwater contamination in more than half of the states. Between 1975 and 1985, fifteen hundred to three thousand public water systems failed to meet safe water standards. Many of these contained unsafe levels of inorganic chemicals and organic chemicals known to be carcinogenic (Rosenbaum 1991).

The potential health effects of water pollution are serious. Nitrates from agricultural runoff can cause birth defects in infants and livestock. Chlorinated solvents from chemical degreasing agents, machinery maintenance, and chemical production are known carcinogens. Trihalomethanes, produced by chemical reactions with chlorinated water, may cause liver and kidney damage and are similarly carcinogenic. Polychlorinated biphenyls (PCBs) are produced as waste from outmoded manufacturing facilities and may cause liver damage and possibly cancer. Lead etching from old piping and solder in water systems may cause nerve damage, learning disabilities, birth defects, and possibly cancer. Coliform and pathogenic bacteria and viruses from leaking sewers and septic tanks spread gastrointestinal illnesses.

Water pollution is, in large part, a result of industrial society. And though the threat to public health has been well documented, economic factors inhibit water quality improvement. The following section looks at the specific tensions between liberalism and water quality.

The Tension between Liberalism and Water Quality

The history of civilization is, in essence, the history of water conflict. Water has been the central resource for all societies, defining where communities can be established, when expanded, and ultimately, when abandoned. Traditional water use was based on a system of riparian rights. Surface waters, such as rivers and steams, were seen as a natural resource beyond ownership. All communities who shared the shoreline had a right to the water. Because communities downstream had the same water rights as those upstream, usage was limited to nondestructive and nondiversionary applications (Boyle, Graves, and Watkins 1971). In this sense, communal good precluded individual ownership.

As agricultural societies gave way to the emerging industrialism of the eighteenth century, concepts of water rights changed. Societies with budding Liberal economies experienced two distinct shifts in thinking. First, property rights became synonymous with individual rights, overshadowing common rights to natural resources. And second, industrial production brought a very different view of nature. Rather than work with the cycles of nature, for mutual benefit, nature was to be subdued by human intervention. Water, then, became seen as property and was used accordingly. The same principle of mineral rights was applied to water rights: "first in time is first in right" (Goldfarb 1988). Through this evolution water rights came to be seen as a property right, defined by ownership. In this way, Liberal society re-

TABLE 5.3. Major Sources of Groundwater Contamination as Reported by States

Source	Number of States Reporting As Source[a]	Number of States Reporting As Primary Source[b]
Septic Tanks	46	9
Underground Storage Tanks	43	13
Agricultural Activities	41	6
On-site Landfills	34	5
Surface Impoundments	33	2
Municipal Landfills	32	1
Abandoned Waste Sites	29	3
Oil and Gas Brine Pits	22	2
Saltwater Intrusion	19	4
Other Landfills	18	0
Road Salting	16	1
Land Application of Sludge	12	0
Regulated Waste Sights	12	1
Mining Activities	11	1
Underground Injection Wells	9	0
Construction Activities	2	0

[a]As reported in 1986 reports to EPA.
[b]Some states did not report a primary source.
Source: Environmental Protection Agency, *Environmental Progress and Challenges: EPA's Update* (Washington DC: EPA, August 1988), 48.

placed communal rights to water resources with individual property rights. The economic character of water rights was legitimized in federal law as the right of prior appropriation.

As water came to be seen as a property right, riparian responsibilities of returning water to its source undiminished and clean were seriously compromised. There was no longer a cultural or legal obligation to maintain water quality for a common good. The implications for water quality are clear. Without a concern for later users "first in time" users had no compulsion to keep water clean nor maintain its flow. The Liberal emphasis on individual good has replaced communal good as the criterion upon which water policy is made. This has made comprehensive clean water policy difficult. Further, capitalism itself has encouraged water degradation. "First in time" ownership rights has allowed the exploitation of water resources for profit maximization.

As corporate capitalism evolved in the United States, riparian water rights became inadequate to support large-scale mining and agriculture. Both operations necessitated diverting large flows of water for irrigation, mineral processing, and ultimately, carrying away wastes. Large-scale water pollution can be traced to the developing industrial economy beginning around 1850. Similarly, sewage became a serious problem with industrial urbanization. For the first time, massive numbers of people were living within the confines of a dense city. Sewage ended up in the same rivers from which populations drew drinking water. And the early brick sewers that were built in cities such as Boston to divert sewage into nearby waterways are, in many cases, still in operation, posing a serious threat to aquifers today.

Legal concepts of prior appropriation encouraged water degradation. By appropriating water resources as one would appropriate property, there was little concern to return water in usable condition. Industry treated water as a property right; it was to be developed, used, and ultimately discarded. By the end of the 1870s there were more than four hundred mining companies in the Sierra Nevadas. Hydraulic equipment allowed these companies to mine huge claims. Canals diverted water from streams and rivers to dammed reservoirs where it was stored. Long flumes carried the water down to nozzles where it was sprayed with tremendous power against the hillsides. Hydraulic mining created massive canyons with widespread erosion and carried silt, sodium chloride, and often heavy metals into the water supply. The mines used almost 72 million gallons a day and created enough runoff to raise stream beds as much as thirty feet (Boyle, Graves, and Watkins 1971).

Until the enactment of the Federal Water Pollution Control Act amendments (the Clean Water Act) in 1972, industrial pollution was simply pumped out with waste water, and in many cases still is. Organic chemical plants and plastics factories create the largest amount of toxic pollution, followed closely by metal finishing, iron, and steel plants. Paper and pulp industries, foundries, and oil refineries also contribute toxins to water (Corson 1990). The Liberal ethic of water as property suggests that "first in time" users are the only users, and consequently there has traditionally been little or no concern for "used" water. Dumping waste water was seen as a right of ownership.

An industrial economy is predicated on the availability of cheap and abundant water. As a consequence, water development policy has been equally vulnerable to economic concerns. By using profit maximization as the criteria for establishing water development projects, liberalism has further contributed to water shortages and the degradation of water quality. California provides a good example. By 1900 California's growing economic interests were concerned about the constraints imposed by a limited water supply. Land developers were concerned about expanding growth, and throughout the state corporate agriculture was concerned about increasing farmable land.

At the turn of the century, the Los Angeles River was supporting a population of one hundred thousand people, a very large community by 1900 standards. City officials, pushed in large part by San Fernando Valley land speculators, financial, and industrial interests, began looking to the Owens Valley to pump water into the southern California basin. To sidestep the objections of Owens Valley farmers the Los Angeles Water Department bought land rights along both sides of the Owens River, thereby obtaining water rights. Through agents, the Los Angeles Water Department discreetly became the largest land owner in the Owens Valley area.

By 1905 the Los Angeles City Council approved a $25 million bond package to finance the construction of an aqueduct to bring Owens Valley water to Los Angeles. A passionate campaign ensued, led in large measure by the *Los Angeles Times*, to convince city residents that Owens Valley water was desperately needed. To heighten concern, several thousand gallons of Los Angeles River water was diverted into sewers, creating the panic of an artificial drought. The bond issue passed, and the Los Angeles Aqueduct was completed in 1913. Owens River water was diverted to Los Angeles, siphoning off the central resource of Owens Valley farmers. The land speculators who had bought up the San Fernando Valley for five to fifteen dollars an acre were now subdividing the land and selling it for as much as one thousand dollars an acre, creating a net profit of between $50 and $100 million dollars (Gottlieb 1988).

Ultimately, the vast development of the southern California suburban mazes created a need for greater water resources than even the Owens Valley Project could provide. In 1927 William Mulholland of the Los Angeles Water and Power District put together a conglomeration of municipal water companies to form the Metropolitan Water District (MWD). Working with the Imperial Valley corporate farms the MWD pushed for a second dam on the Colorado. The Swing-Johnson Bill (1928) authorized the construction of Boulder Dam as a storage facility. Imperial Dam, and the All-American Canal were to replace the inadequate Imperial Canal. In 1931 southern California voters passed a $220 million bond issue to build the Colorado River Aqueduct to bring Colorado River water to southern California faucets.

As agribusiness in California's central valley depleted groundwater stores, there was increased political pressure to divert Sacramento River water to supplement the smaller San Joaquin River. The central valley, along with the Imperial Valley, is one of the most fertile areas in the country but lacks adequate rainfall. The arid climate allows for a yearlong growing season, but only if cheap and abundant water can be imported. Agricultural interests were successful in pressing for the Central Valley Project (CVP). Ultimately financed by the federal government, the CVP created Shasta Dam and a series of canals that doubled California's irrigatable land from 4.9 million acres to 8.6 million acres.

By the 1950s large landowners on the west side of the central valley, who were not connected to the CVP, sought their own cheap water. Kern corporate farmers, led by the huge Kern County Land Company, along with several oil companies and the growing MWD pushed for a new water project that would benefit them. Their efforts resulted in the State Water Project, funded by a 1960 bond issue supplying $1.75 billion.

Large agriculture has always been the greatest consumer of water, using 82 percent of the state's supply in an average year (Vershner 1991). By diverting water west from the Colorado River and south from the Sacramento Delta, agribusiness has been able to convert the arid central valley and the southeastern state into one of the most profitable cropland areas of the country, often growing water-intensive crops such as rice and alfalfa. Similarly, the Owens Valley and Colorado River water projects that were pushed through by real estate and financial speculators enabled residential development of southern California at a substantial profit. The sprawling suburban growth of southern California is directly tied to the water diverted south through the Los Angeles Aqueduct and west through the Colorado River Aqueduct (Gottlieb 1988).

Water availability in California has always been more a function of management than nature. The major water suppliers of the state, such as the massive Metropolitan Water District in southern California, are water wholesalers—selling water to local water companies—created to deliver cheap and abundant water. When rainfall is below average the water companies rely on stored-water sources. When drought cycles periodically hit the state, the response is not to conserve but to acquire new sources. Consequently, though there was below-average rainfall each year between 1985 and 1992, water cutbacks were rejected by water managers until 1991. The cycle of water crises in California is a direct result of a refusal to impose early limitations (O'Brien 1992).

By viewing water as property, to be disposed of according to economic criteria, rather than as a communal resource, California water development has been exceedingly shortsighted. The redistribution of water resources favors, almost without exception, those interests that are best able to cultivate the requisite political resources. The Kern and Imperial Valley corporate farms, the Metropolitan Water District, large land developers, industry, and oil companies all benefit from the diversion of water.

California water policy has been vulnerable both to the intensive lobbying efforts of corporate PACs and to the domination of legislative committees by pro-agriculture representatives. In the 1990 to 1992 state assembly, for example, seven of the thirteen members of the assembly Water, Parks, and Wildlife Committee were also members of the assembly Agriculture Committee. Six were from rural agricultural districts. And, not surprisingly, ten of the twelve members of the assembly Agriculture Committee, which also maintains jurisdiction over water policy, represented agricultural districts, mostly in the central valley (*California Journal* 1991). Those interests that have little or no representation suffer. The local farmers of the Owens Valley were ruined, and farmers in Mexico who rely on the Colorado are left with a heavily salted murky creek.

In November 1992 an innovative approach to water policy was signed into federal law. The Central Valley Project Improvement Act creates a system of marketable water rights for farmers using California's Central Valley Project. This system encourages farmers to conserve in two ways: first, a system of tiered pricing was instituted to punish excessive use; and second, central valley farmers can sell a portion of their water rights. While not dismantling water subsidies, central valley farmers would pay a greater share of costs—more expensive water should result in conservation. In addition, the act sets aside a greater share of water for residential and municipal consumption, thus minimizing some of the tension that exists between corporate agriculture and municipal water agencies. Finally, the act creates a reserve of eight hundred thousand acre feet (approximately 10 percent of CVP water) for protection and restoration of wetlands (Schneider 1992; Postel 1993).

However innovative water marketing may be, marketing water rights does not solve the tension between liberalism and water quality management. Federal water is still highly subsidized, thus the "market" value of the water does not reflect the actual cost. By the mid-1980s, central valley farmers had only paid 4 percent of actual project costs—$38 million of the $950 million invested—the rest came from federal subsidies (Postel 1993). Further, while placing a greater burden of cost on CVP users will create an economic incentive for conservation, that incentive is minimal when compared to the actual subsidies federal taxpayers are providing. A more aggressive water policy might dictate the type of crops that would be eligible for federal support. Specifically, subsidizing the growing of water-intensive crops like rice and alfalfa in the central valley simply makes no sense. In regions where water is scarce, and growing urban areas compete with agriculture, individual self-interest becomes a poor mechanism for determining water use. A comprehensive water policy is best created with a common interest in mind. Creating a market for water rights to ensure conservation only makes sense when considering the individual user; if individual self-interest were replaced with regional self-interest, water policy might more effectively manage long-term water development and use. While many argue that the federal government has no business dictating what types of crops farmers can grow, the federal government also has no responsibility to provide farmers with subsidized water. Consequently, if the federal government is a partner in agriculture, through its water investment, then it indeed has a role to play in determining sustainable crop management.

The consequences of using economic development as the determining factor in creating water policy are serious. In addition to water shortages, the diversion of water has caused severe ecological damage. The shifting of water flows has changed climates and habitats. The result of constant watering and irrigation has been a measurable increase in humidity, which in turn has shifted wildlife habitats. The damming of rivers has permanently blocked freshwater fish, such as salmon, access to spawning regions, and flooded spawning beds and warmer water temperatures caused by slowed water movement has further inhibited spawning.

Water storage made possible by damming encourages wasteful water usage, with potentially harmful side effects. Over irrigation, for example, washes salts, minerals, pesticides, and fertilizers back into water sources. In the Colorado's Grand Valley, federally subsidized water is so inexpensive that flood irrigation is used, washing approximately three hundred thousand tons of mineral salts and toxins into the Colorado River, threatening Los Angeles drinking water (Rosenbaum 1985). The diversion of water creates both flooded canyons in some areas and low water levels in other areas. Water quality is directly related to quantity, as low water levels exacerbate pollution problems. As water levels fall, pollutants will accumulate in greater concentrations in the water that remains. Moreover, depleted aquifers in coastal areas allow seawater to seep into groundwater.

The relationship between economic concerns and water quality is important. As water rights came to be seen as property rights, water "owners" had little compulsion to maintain water quality. And, of course, it is significantly cheaper to dump waste back into the water supply than to either clean wastewater or prevent that waste in the first place. Billions of gallons of pollutants are regularly discharged into municipal sewers. Of the three hundred thousand industries that regularly discharge waste into surface waters, only 15 percent are regulated by state or federal discharge permits (Rosenbaum 1991:41; *New York Times* 1988a).

Federal water policy has sought to solve the problem of pollution by establishing water quality standards. But, as the next section discusses, water policy suffers from many of the same problems as air policy.

Water Policy and Symbolic Politics

The history of water development is, as the California example illustrates, a history of elite policy domination. Policy elites have claimed that water development has been the result of democratic politics, but in fact, it came as a result of elite manipulation of public opinion, largely through creating perceptions of water shortages. At the same time, as a result of high public anxiety over water pollution, policy elites have marketed water policy as bold regulation, satisfying public demand, though the policies themselves are problematic: enforcement is weak and discretionary; standards are weak; and only a fraction of waterborne pollutants are monitored. Like air policy, water policy echoes Edelman's (1977) notion of "words that succeed and policies that fail."

The history of water policy is similar to that of air policy. As the two most immediate and important resources for human survival, air and water make up the two major arenas of environmental policy. Federal water policy predates air policy, though each follows a similar evolution. As Table 5.4 illustrates, early water policy focused first on research, later on federal subsidies to encourage action, and finally on command and control policies. And, like the Clean Air Act, water policy has experienced a retreat in commitment from federal regulators since its peak in 1972. Water quality has not improved significantly since 1972 (Kraft and Vig 1990).

Clean Water Policy

Water policy attacks pollution according to water category, with the strongest standards aimed at protecting surface waters. Unlike the health-based "ambient standards" established for air quality, water quality is based on "effluent standards," relying on currently available control technologies (Kenski and Ingram 1986). The Federal Water Pollution Control Act amendments (FWPCAA, 1972) sought to eliminate the "discharge of pollutants" into navigable U.S. waters by 1985, with

TABLE 5.4. Evolution of Federal Water Policy

Legislation Adopted	Specific Provisions
1899 The Refuse Act	Barred discharge or deposit of refuse in navigable waters without permit.
1948 Water Pollution Control Act	Authorized Public Health Service to research water pollution.
1956 Water Pollution Control Act Amendments	Provided $50 million in grants for waste treatment plant construction in small cities. Authorized states to establish water quality criteria. Created conference procedure to publicize interstate problem.
1965 Water Quality Act	Required states to establish water standards; allowed Health, Education, and Welfare to set standards if states failed to do so.
1972 Federal Water Pollution Control Act Amendments (Clean Water Act)	National technology based effluent standards and established discharge limits for categories of sources. National pollution permit system allowed regulation of noncompliant sources.
1974 Safe Drinking Water Act	Required EPA to establish safe drinking water standards for twenty-six major pollutants.
1977 Clean Water Act Amendments	Created a larger role for states in establishing priorities for waste treatment. Postponed deadlines established in the 1972 act. Increased control of the toxic pollutants.
1981 Municipal Wastewater Construction Grant Amendments	Reduced share of federal Financing of municipal sewage treatment.
1987 Water Quality Act	Further postponed deadlines established in the 1972 act.

Sources: Table 1, Kenski and Ingram (1986); Table 4.1, Freeman (1990).

an interim goal of attaining water quality that would support fish and recreation by 1983 (Rosenbaum 1991).

Specifically, the amendments, along with the Water Quality Act (1987), require that states, with EPA guidance, establish water quality standards according to water use—recreation, fishing, irrigation, and waste disposal. The legislation also required the EPA to establish effluent standards according to the "best practical control technology currently available" which were to be met by 1979, and the "best available technology economically achievable" by 1983. All municipal sources were required to achieve "secondary treatment levels" by 1977 and effluent levels based on the "best practical technology" by 1983. New nonmunicipal sources are required to use the "best available demonstrated control technology." Further, the legislation prohibited the discharge of any pollutant into any sewer system. Pretreatment standards require industry to treat discharge before dumping. Finally, FWPCAA authorized $18 billion in grants for assisting local communities in building water treatment facilities (Kenski and Ingram 1986; Rosenbaum 1991).

Enforcement of water quality regulation is based on the EPA administrator's discretion in delegating enforcement responsibilities to states. The states, in turn, issue discharge permits specifying allowable discharge to all waste-producing facilities. The 1987 amendments require states to create plans for EPA approval outlining how nonpoint sources (such as urban runoff or agriculture) will be brought into compliance.

Groundwater protection has traditionally been seen by federal authorities as a state and local problem. FWPCAA has an impact on groundwater indirectly, by limiting pollutants that may seep into groundwater sources. The Safe Drinking Water Act (1974, amendments 1976) required the EPA to establish safe water standards for twenty-six major pollutants. Though the EPA reports that almost 90 percent of community water systems meet standards, several communities remain out of compliance (Rosenbaum 1991). Several other pieces of federal legislation affect groundwater to a smaller extent, including the Resource Conservation and Recovery Act (1976) and Superfund (1980) (see Chapter 6). On the whole, however, groundwater remains the domain of the state and lacks adequate federal protection.

Like air policy, water policy has been marketed as a vigorous attempt on the part of government to protect the nation's water resources. In fact, however, water policy is seriously flawed. The current model of federal water policy grew out of a desire to satisfy public demand for improved environmental conditions in the early 1970s.

The Symbolic Content of Water Policy

Public awareness of water pollution is limited to the extremes. Only when raw sewage floats by, or when tap water is distasteful, discolored, or odorous does public concern become aroused. The mysterious and cloistered arena in which water policy is made allows policy elites to claim that substantial progress is being made. While poor air quality can typically be recognized by citizens, poor water quality often cannot. The most dangerous pollutants (e.g., fecal coliform bacteria, lead, PCBs, and chlorinated solvents) are invisible to the eye. Public concern, therefore, is abstract and easily reassured with regulatory promises.

The symbolic aspects of water policy are similar to those of air policy. Both followed mass public demand for improved environmental conditions. And both air and water policies were enacted with strong standards and strict deadlines—even though few legislators expected compliance. Clean water policies focus on establishing standards requiring expensive control technologies and then inviting voluntary compliance, resulting in what can only be called regulatory stalemate.

Enforcement, the keystone to any viable policy, is severely limited by the EPA's inability to staff programs. By 1988, for example, the EPA only had a staff of forty-five to monitor the two hundred thousand public water systems covered by the Safe Drinking Water Act (Rosenbaum 1991:33; *New York Times* 1988b). Furthermore, the water quality standards themselves are problematic. Only a small number of chemicals that are thought to pollute groundwater are monitored. The EPA's water quality indices are measured mainly on only six pollutants: fecal coliform bacteria; dissolved oxygen; total phosphorus; total mercury; total lead; and biochemical oxygen demand. Water quality measurements often exclude heavy metals, synthetic organic compounds (including solvents and PCBs), and dissolved solids (Rosenbaum 1991; GAO 1986a). Hazardous and toxic wastes percolating down from disposal sites, and heavy metals etching from piping pose serious health risks but are outside of policy limits.

Charles City, Iowa, provides one example. Salsbury Laboratories, a small veterinary pharmaceutical company, had for a generation been dumping its chemical waste in an eight-acre gravel pit. Though several private wells adjacent to the site were found to be contaminated in the 1950s, there was no general concern. But, in 1969, Samuel Tuthill, director of the Iowa Geological Survey, wrote Iowa's Water Pollution Control Commission that arsenic compounds were present in the Cedar River nearby and the Cedar Aquifer, which supplied water to more than three hundred thousand people. The data implicated the Salsbury dump. But the warning was ignored. Salsbury argued that there was no proof of injury or death from its waste and that the $20 million it would cost to clean the site was prohibitive. The lab continued dumping for eight more years. Between 1953 and 1977 approximately 1 million cubic feet of arsenic wastes had been dumped in the site, contaminating 30 million cubic feet of soil. EPA documents show that the agency had been aware of the hazard since 1972, but had taken no action. Ultimately, in 1977, after discovering trace chemicals in Waterloo fifty miles away, the Iowa Department of Environmental Quality ordered the firm to stop its dumping. By 1979, Salsbury proposed to clean the site by covering it with topsoil to divert runoff and reduce leachate. Ten years after state officials first became aware of the health risk, the site remained in place (Brown 1980).

Although this scenario has played itself out in thousands of towns throughout the country, federal policy has left cleanup to the states. The only program that authorizes federal action is Superfund, but this requires the site to be identified as among the most severe waste hazards in the country. Of the estimated 425,000 sites around the country, the EPA has identified only 1,236 for immediate attention (GAO 1987; EPA 1989b; EPA 1991).

In short, existing water policy standards are weak and enforcement is lax. Even when hazardous pollution is identified, federal authorities are slow to act. This is not merely an issue of policy implementation falling short. Rather, it is an example of how symbolic policy has replaced substantive regulation. Clean water policy has been established largely to satisfy public demand. The permit system is only weakly enforced, and only a fraction of pollutants are monitored. Since 1972, when the Clean Water Act was passed, water quality has shown little or no improvement. And in perhaps the most blatant symbolic aspect of the clean water debate, the EPA has released misleading data on water improvement. In summarizing a state survey of designated water use in 1988, the EPA reported water quality in gross percentages, even though the data were incomplete. The survey included only 21 percent of the nation's stream miles, 32 percent of lake acres, and only 55 percent of marine estuarine miles (Rosenbaum 1991:199). Water policy has eased public arousal but has failed to improve water quality— "words that succeed and policies that fail" (Edelman 1977).

Conclusion

As a result of viewing water as property to be regulated by economic concerns, Liberal society has replaced communal good with individual good as the criterion for developing water access and maintaining water quality. In characterizing water as a commodity to be exploited for maximum profit, like any other mineral resource, liberalism has turned traditional riparian water rights on its ear. Water users have little or no responsibility to assure that water, once used, maintains its purity.

This chapter has explored the tension between liberalism and water use. Specifically, the transition of water rights from its riparian roots to its current definition as an appropriated property right has replaced communal good with individual (and corporate) good in determining water allocation and quality. Further, capitalism encourages water degradation by legitimizing dumping as a cost-effective solution for wastewater disposal. The chapter concluded by arguing that water policy has sought to ease the tension between liberalism and water quality through symbolic action. The following chapter applies the analysis to solid and hazardous waste policy.

6   The Politics of Waste

Waste continues to be one of the most serious problems facing Liberal society. Our consumer economy encourages wasteful habits: disposable products of every sort, planned obsolescence of appliances and equipment, and the over packaging of consumer goods, to name but a few. On average, each American throws out more than 3.5 pounds of "trash" every day, a total of nearly 10 billion tons per year (O'Leary 1988). The United States recycles only 11 percent of its waste, compared with 30 percent in western Europe and nearly 50 percent in Japan. The waste problem has an impact on the environment on every level: toxic leachate percolates into groundwater; the sheer volume of solid waste threatens to overwhelm limited landfill space; and the cycle of disposable products creates an increasing need for raw materials.

Waste presents a special challenge to Liberal society. The Liberal emphasis on economic expansion has resulted in an ever-increasing amount of waste. The constant drive to maximize profits creates an economic incentive to find the cheapest production and waste disposal methods, which, typically, are the least environmentally friendly. And, the need for constant sales encourages the disposability of consumer goods. Rather than attack the waste problem at its root, through waste reduction, existing policy merely attempts to regulate disposal. As a result, waste policy is more symbolic than substantive. This chapter examines the tensions between liberalism and waste management.

Background: Solid and Hazardous Waste

The Resource Conservation and Recovery Act (RCRA) includes in its definition of solid waste garbage, sludge, and solids and liquids from industrial, commercial, mining, agricultural, and community activities (including wastewater). In short, all discarded materials, excluding domestic sewage, are defined as solid waste, from municipal trash to agricultural runoff. The United States creates 10 billion metric tons of solid waste annually. And as Table 6.1 illustrates, the amount per capita of solid waste produced each year is increasing. Industrial processes account for 65 percent of waste, the production and use of oil and gas accounts for 20 percent, and mining accounts for 12 percent. Municipal garbage (nonsewage waste) accounts for only 1 percent of all solid waste, producing 167 million tons annually (Council on Environmental Quality 1990).

Industrial waste, typically, is disposed of in private facilities. Salvage yards separate marketable materials and dispose of remaining waste in landfills, and to a much lesser extent, through incineration (EPA 1988a). Wastewater and agricultural runoff are disposed of directly into surface waters, with little or no treatment (see Chapter 5). Municipal waste is disposed of primarily through landfills, with only 11 percent recycled and 80 percent buried (U.S. Bureau of the Census 1989). Municipal waste is expected to increase by 20 percent by the year 2000 (EPA 1988b). As Table 6.2 illustrates, municipal waste is made up primarily of paper products. Fifty percent of volume and 30 percent of weight is made up of discarded packaging of food and consumer products (Pollock 1987).

Solid waste disposal poses a variety of problems. First and foremost, the burying of solid waste is quickly using up the scarce landfill space available. Of the twenty thousand landfills in use in 1978, only six

TABLE 6.1 Municipal Solid Waste Generation and Recovery, 1960–1990

Year	Gross Discards per capita	total	Materials Recovery per capita	total	Recovery Energy	Net Discards
1960	2.65	87.5	0.18	5.8	0	81.7
1965	2.88	102.3	0.17	6.2	0.2	95.9
1970	3.22	120.5	0.21	8.0	0.4	112.1
1975	3.18	125.3	0.23	9.1	0.7	115.5
1980	3.43	142.6	0.32	13.4	2.7	126.5
1985	3.49	152.5	0.35	15.3	7.6	129.7
1990	3.67	167.4	0.40	18.4	13.3	135.7

a) per capita reported in pounds per day
b) totals reported in million tons
c) 1990 data are projections
Source: U.S. Environmental Protection Agency; *Environmental Quality* (1990:492).

TABLE 6.2. Municipal Waste Composition 1986

Paper and paperboard	35.6%
Yard Waste	20.1%
Food Waste	8.9%
Metals	8.9%
Glass	8.4%
Plastics	7.3%
Wood	4.1%
Rubber and leather	2.8%
Textiles	2.0%
Other	1.8%

Source: Franklin Associates, 1988, *Characterization of Municipal Solid Waste in the U.S., 1960–2000* (Prairie Village, KS: March).

thousand were still in use in 1988. This number is expected to drop to four thousand by the end of 1993, and one thousand by 2005 (Corson 1990). New landfills are expensive and difficult to site due to NIMBY-ism (Not in My Back Yard). Citizens simply do not want landfills in their communities.

Further, landfills present environmental dangers. As rain seeps through landfills, toxins are leached from waste material and percolate into groundwater. Methane is produced as a byproduct of decomposing waste and if left uncontrolled creates the potential for explosion. Currently, only about 15 percent of landfills are lined, 5 percent collect leachate, 25 percent monitor groundwater, and only around one hundred sites collect methane (Corson 1990). Incineration, similarly, releases hazardous chemicals such as dioxins into the air, and toxic ash must then be buried in a landfill.

Hazardous and toxic wastes are distinguished from solid waste by their toxicity. The Toxic Substances Control Act (TSCA) and RCRA define "hazardous" materials as those materials which pose a threat to humans and the environment. "Toxic" materials are defined as those materials that are deadly to living organisms, causing neurological damage, or lung, liver, kidney, immune system, or fetal damage (Council on Environmental Quality 1979; Rosenbaum 1991).

While many substances are clearly toxic by TSCA and RCRA definitions, the precise line between "hazardous" and "toxic" materials is somewhat ambiguous. This ambiguity combines with the economic impact that a "toxic" label would carry, to create the politicization of the hazardous/toxic determination (Rosenbaum 1991). "Toxic" substances are regulated more stringently than "hazardous" materials, and consumers tend to avoid "toxic" products. As a result of the potential loss in sales a "toxic" label might create, manufacturers lobby the EPA intensively. But, regardless of the agency distinction, both "hazardous" and "toxic" substances present serious public health risks.

Hazardous and toxic materials permeate our society. Seventy thousand chemicals are currently in use in the United States, with as many as fifteen hundred new chemicals being introduced annually (Rosenbaum 1991). Chemical manufacturers and processors produce 80 percent of the nation's hazardous waste (Conservation Foundation 1987). The health effects of exposure to toxic and hazardous substances include cancer, fetal damage, autoimmune depression, damage to blood forming organs, and brain damage, all of which may lead to death. Table 6.3 reviews the source and specific health effects of the most common toxic substances.

Less than 10 percent of the nation's annual 260 million metric tons of hazardous waste has been disposed of properly, making unsafe hazardous waste sites a major problem (Rosenbaum 1991; WRI and IIED 1987). Approximately 65 percent of hazardous waste is disposed of through landfills, injection wells, and surface ponds. Twenty-two percent is released into sewers or directly into surface waters. Only 1 percent is recycled or processed to reduce toxicity before discharge (Corson 1990). The General Accounting Office (GAO) estimates that there may be as many as 425,000 waste sites around the country (GAO 1987). The EPA has identified 1,236 sites requiring immediate attention in its 1991 Superfund National Priority List (Viviano 1991; EPA 1989b). As Table 6.4 identifies, there are sites in every state.

The EPA estimates that toxins seep into groundwater at three-fourths of the sites (Weber 1988). The impact of hazardous waste on public health can be serious. In Woburn, Massachusetts, where industrial solvents have seeped into the water supply, the child leukemia rate is eight times the national average (Weisskopf 1986). The best-known incident of exposure to hazardous waste was Love Canal. In the 1940s Love Canal was an open pit used as a dumping facility. Forty thousand tons of toxic waste, including carcinogens, were dumped into the canal. The site was ultimately filled in and sold to the local Board of Education. In 1977 the site began leaking, forcing the evacuation of more than two hundred families (*Washington Post* 1988). Love Canal became a national symbol of poor toxic waste management, focusing media attention on abandoned waste sites throughout the United States. This media attention combined with the growing environmental movement to force a legislative response. By 1980 Congress authorized Superfund to finance the cleanup of especially dangerous abandoned sites.

TABLE 6.3 Source and Health Effects of Selected Hazardous and Toxic Substances

Substance	Common Sources	Health Effect
DDT	pesticide	cancer; liver damage; fetal damage; damages bird eggs
BHC	pesticide	cancer; fetal damage
Benzene	solvents, pharmaceuticals, detergent production, gasoline	headaches; nausea; loss of muscle coordination; leukemia; bone marrow damage
Vinyl Chloride	plastics production	lung and liver cancer; depresses central nervous system; suspected embryo toxin
Dioxin	herbicides, waste incineration	cancer; birth defects; skin disease
PCBs	Electronics, hydraulic fluid, fluorescent lighting	skin damage; possible digestive damage; possible carcinogen
Lead	paint, gasoline, car batteries	neurotoxin; headaches; mental impairment in children; brain, liver, and kidney damage
Cadmium	zinc processing, batteries, fertilizer processing	cancer in animals; liver and kidney damage

Source: World Resources Institute and International Institute for Environment and Development, 1987, *World Resources 1987* (New York: Basic Books, Inc.).

The Tension between Liberalism and Waste Management

Capitalism, as an economic system establishing supply and distribution of goods, is largely inconsistent with waste management. It is the emphasis on productivity that creates the dilemma for waste management. Liberal society defines economic success as an ever growing GNP. There is constant pressure, consequently, to increase market share, resulting in greater production of goods. The plentiful economy encour-

TABLE 6.4 Superfund National Priority List, 1991

State	Number of Existing Sites	Sites Previously Cleaned
New Jersey	112	3
Pennsylvania	101	6
California	88	0
New York	84	0
Michigan	79	2
Florida	54	3
Washington	46	1
Minnesota	38	1
Wisconsin	39	0
Illinois	38	1
Indiana	35	2
Ohio	33	1
Texas	30	1
Massachusetts	25	1
Missouri	24	0
South Carolina	22	0
North Carolina	23	1
Iowa	21	0
Delaware	21	1
Virginia	21	1
Kentucky	17	0
Colorado	16	0
New Hampshire	16	0
Connecticut	14	1
Tennessee	14	1
Georgia	14	1
Alabama	12	0
Oklahoma	10	0
Utah	12	0
Arizona	12	1
Arkansas	10	0
Kansas	11	0
Louisiana	11	0
Rhode Island	11	0
Maryland	12	2
Montana	10	0
New Mexico	10	0
Idaho	9	0
Maine	9	0
Puerto Rico	9	0

(continued)

TABLE 6.4 (*Continued*)

State	Number of Existing Sites	Sites Previously Cleaned
Oregon	8	0
Vermont	8	0
Hawaii	7	0
Alaska	6	1
Nebraska	6	0
West Virginia	5	0
Mississippi	3	1
South Dakota	3	0
Wyoming	3	0
North Dakota	2	0
Guam	1	0
Nevada	1	0
American Samoa	1	0
Commonwealth of Marianas	0	0
District of Columbia	0	0
Trust Territories	0	0
Virgin Islands	0	0
Total:	1,236	

Sources: Environmental Protection Agency 1991;
San Francisco Chronicle, May 29, 1991, A4.

ages disposable goods; the usable life of products is necessarily short, to allow for continued demand for new and improved products. Aggressive marketing techniques have resulted in over packaging of consumer goods that manufacturers hope will make their product stand out. As mentioned earlier, fifty percent of landfill volume is made up of discarded packaging (Pollock 1987). As technology has allowed for more cost efficient production methods, it has become cheaper in many cases to simply replace consumer products rather than to fix them.

As Table 6.5 illustrates, there is a correlation between GNP growth and the per capita increase in municipal solid waste since 1960. The average person throws out more than three and one-half pounds of trash per day, compared with two and one-half pounds per day in 1960 (Council on Environmental Quality 1990). The result is a consumer economy that has a continuously increasing amount of waste of which

TABLE 6.5 GNP and Municipal Solid Waste Increase 1960–1990

Year	GNP (billions of 1982 dollars)	Municipal Solid Waste (million tons)	Municipal Waste per Capita (pounds per day)
1960	1665.3	87.5	2.65
1965	2087.6	102.3	2.88
1970	2416.2	120.5	3.22
1975	2695.0	125.3	3.18
1980	3187.1	142.6	3.43
1985	3618.7	152.5	3.49
1990	4155.8	167.4	3.67

Sources: Executive Office of the President, Council of Economic Advisers, 1990, *1990 Economic Report* (Washington, DC: GPO); Environmental Protection Agency, Office of Solid Waste and Emergency Response, 1990, *Characterization of Municipal Solid Waste in the United States, 1960–2000* (Prairie Village, KS: Franklin Associates); U.S. Department of Energy, Energy Information Administration, 1992, *International Energy Annual 1990* (Washington, DC: GPO).

to dispose. The expansive emphasis of capitalism breeds an anticonservationist ethic.

The tension between liberalism and environmental quality is felt strongly in the area of toxic waste. Industry must often choose between public good and private profit. On the one hand, industrial production produces waste by-products—many of them toxic. On the other, maximizing profit requires cost-efficient production methods and disposal techniques—and ever growing sales. The net result is the production of vast amounts of industrial waste that must be disposed of. The classic Liberal debate between communal good and private profit is better understood in the context of waste management. Toxic waste disposal provides a good illustration.

Toxic Waste Disposal

The Hooker Chemical Company was established in 1906 by Elon Huntington Hooker, as a small chemical company specializing in producing caustic soda from salt brine. By 1940 the company produced chlorine and several related products, with $20 million in annual sales. The company was bought by Armand Hammer's Occidental Petroleum in 1968. And, by 1978, the company's annual sales reached $1.7 billion. Hooker Chemical was a classic American success story, growing continuously and coming to provide a financial backbone to several communities in

the Northeast and Midwest. But by 1978 the underbelly of the beast began to show itself (Brown 1980).

Hooker Chemical operated a facility near the Niagara River in up-
state New York. Between 1940 and 1953 the company used a half-mile
trench, Love Canal, as a basin for its caustic waste. In 1953 the company
filled in the basin and sold it to a local school district as a school site for
one dollar and an agreement releasing Hooker of all liability that might
arise. By the 1970s chemical waste had leached into the adjacent aquifer
and chemical sludge seeped into basements of nearby homes. Ultimately, several cases of birth defects, cancer, and other diseases were
tied to the site, and the state of New York stepped in to evacuate 239
families. The ensuing media uproar made Love Canal a household
word and brought the fears of chemical contamination to communities
throughout the United States. But while many observers may have seen
Love Canal as an isolated event, it was only one of a series of catastrophes (Moskowitz, et al., 1982; Brown 1980).

In the early 1960s, another Hooker plant was burying its waste in
a dump site adjacent to Bloody Run, a small tributary of the Niagara. By
1963, several local citizens, particularly children, were complaining of
respiratory problems, but the state Department of Environmental Conservation maintained there was no contamination. As late as 1973 a regional inspector came out and without testing the water claimed it was
pure, even though seepage from the site periodically gave the water an
orange-red appearance. In July 1978, Michael Brown, the journalist who
covered Love Canal, had water and mud from Bloody Run tested. The
lab found traces of lindane, C-56, PCBs, DDT, Mirex, and several other
chlorinated hydrocarbons. The water was so contaminated that the lab
advised Brown not to touch it again (Brown 1980).

As a result of the bad publicity over Love Canal, Occidental announced that it would cap the site with clay to prevent runoff from
seeping through the site. But this did little for the existing leachate and
offered no protection from future geologic movement. Hooker estimated that eighty thousand tons of highly toxic waste was dumped at
Bloody Run, including thirty-three hundred tons of trichlorophenal
(the precursor to dioxin)—sixteen times the amount at Love Canal
(Brown 1980).

Between 1947 and 1975 the Hooker Chemical Company know-
ingly buried tens of thousands of tons of toxics immediately adjacent to
the water supply of one hundred thousand people. Sludge from the local drinking water treatment plant was found to contain traces of Mirex,
C-56, benzene derivatives, and other toxins. Cancer levels in Niagara
County between 1973 and 1975 were well above average. According to

New York's Cancer Control Bureau, lung and bronchus cancer was 38 percent above the state average, leukemia was 55 percent above average, kidney cancer was 44 percent above average, pancreatic cancer was 27 percent above average, and stomach cancer was 20 percent above average (Brown 1980:80).

This pattern began emerging at Hooker plants throughout the United States. In Montague, Michigan, Hooker simply dumped C-56 waste in its back lots, which percolated directly into nearby water sources. Hooker knew that its sludge lagoons were contaminating groundwater, and when pressed, Duane Colpoys, the site manager, told the Michigan Department of Natural Resources (DNR) that there were only "maybe ten or twenty" drums spread around the back area. When the DNR finally inspected the site the following year, they found more than twenty thousand fifty-five-gallon drums of toxic waste leaking into the ground. In White Springs, Florida, a Hooker phosphorus plant routinely released as much as three thousand pounds of fluoride into the air, when only thirty-four pounds were permitted to be released in any single day. In Houston, Texas, a Hooker plant switched to a cheaper phosphoric acid process even though company officials knew it would release more fluoride than regulations allowed. And in Lathrop, California, a Hooker plant had dumped fertilizer and nitrates into an unlined pond, contaminating wells within a three-mile radius (Brown 1980).

While Hooker may have had the misfortune of media attention, thousands of other companies also consciously put aside public good in order to maximize profit. This is, in a sense, the flipside of the American dream. Liberalism's emphasis on private good creates an economic incentive to create and dump waste. Clearly, the Hooker Chemical Company and others like it routinely place their corporate self-interest above the communal interests of the society around them. But in so doing these companies are simply acting according to Liberal assumptions.

The Hooker experience illustrates the tensions between liberalism and waste management well. In pursuing its own corporate self-interest, Hooker chose the cheapest production and waste disposal methods, successfully maximizing its profit—albeit at the expense of the community at large. To some degree, the Hobson's choice facing Hooker and other companies—between corporate self-interest and communal good—is the choice facing Liberal society at large: is it possible to maintain communal interests while maximizing private good? Hooker's actions offer one answer. But Liberal society has not yet accepted the parameters of the dilemma. The following section explores the role waste policy plays in obfuscating this crucial question.

Waste Policy and Symbolic Politics

Like the other environmental policy areas, waste management policies arrived late. Until the mid-1970s municipalities, industries, and farms simply buried or burned their waste. The impact of widespread landfill use was not understood until recently, nor was the ecological cycle of dependency. In the late 1970s three programs were enacted to deal with the growing waste problem: the Resource Conservation and Recovery Act; the Toxic Substances Control Act; and Superfund.

The Resource Conservation and Recovery Act (RCRA) enacted in 1976 sought to define and control solid waste for the first time, through regulation and ultimately through conservation. RCRA affected the disposal of all "solid waste," defined as any waste solids, liquids, sludge (excluding sewage), and contained gases. The act mandated criteria for safe disposal. The EPA was ordered to issue regulations defining minimum safety standards for disposal sites and was ordered to publish a list of all facilities failing to meet these standards.

RCRA required the EPA to regulate hazardous waste by defining explicitly criteria for recognizing hazardous substances and listing specific materials known to be hazardous. A manifest system was authorized to track hazardous substances from origin to disposal. RCRA created a permit system allowing only those industries which meet safe disposal guidelines to operate.

To promote conservation RCRA required the Commerce Department to promote the commercial viability of waste recovery (recycling). This included encouraging markets for recycled materials, encouraging the development of waste recovery technologies, and encouraging research into conservation. The cornerstone of RCRA was to be waste reduction and safe disposal.

The Toxic Substances Control Act (1976) and its 1986 amendments regulate the manufacture and distribution of chemical substances. TSCA has five objectives: collect information; screen new chemicals; test chemicals; control chemicals; and control asbestos. TSCA ordered the EPA to issue regulations requiring chemical producers to keep records on the health effects of chemicals and to submit product information to the EPA administrator, including formula, product uses, and adverse health effects. The EPA publishes these data in a directory of all existing chemicals. Manufacturers are required to notify the EPA at least ninety days prior to commercially releasing any new chemical to allow the agency to screen new substances. TSCA empowers the EPA to temporarily suspend production of any new chemical if insufficient information has been provided to allow screening. The EPA is empowered to suspend permanently any new chemical found to present an "unreasonable risk of injury to health or the environment." TSCA requires producers to test chemicals based on recommendations from the Interagency Testing Committee, which is comprised of representatives from eight federal agencies. Further, the act requires the EPA to control any substance found to present an "unreasonable risk." This control can range from requiring a warning label to an outright ban. Finally, the act requires the EPA to develop a program to inspect for asbestos-containing materials in public school buildings and to remove any asbestos found.

Superfund was created specifically to fund the cleanup of abandoned toxic waste sites. Authorized under the Comprehensive Environmental Response, Compensation, and Liability Act of 1980 (CERCLA, PL-510), Superfund was passed in the midst of growing public concern following Love Canal. The legislation required hazardous waste site operators to disclose the content of their buried wastes to the EPA by June 1981. The EPA, in turn, was required to use this information to create a national site list. As well, the EPA was ordered to create a national priority list of waste sites requiring federal cleanup. The EPA was authorized to clean leaking sites if the owner failed to do so or could not be found. The liability for cleanup fell on those responsible for releasing the hazardous substances. In order to do this, Superfund authorized $1.6 billion to finance the removal and cleanup of the site. Eighty-six percent of the fund was to come from a tax on petro and organic chemical producers, processors, and importers.

By the mid 1980s it was becoming evident that the initial authorization was far too little and the number of abandoned sites was severely underestimated. The Bhopal disaster in 1984 refocused congressional attention to toxic cleanup, and by 1986 Superfund was reauthorized in the Superfund Amendments and Reauthorization Act (SARA). An additional $8.5 billion was authorized for site cleanup and $500 million for cleaning underground liquid storage tanks (e.g., leaking gasoline tanks at filling stations). The amendments mandated that cleanup projects use the "best available technologies" or existing state standards when more stringent. As well, the amendments required that the public be informed of cleanup activities and be invited to participate through community hearings. Finally, with Bhopal in mind, the amendments required that detailed information on all chemicals made, stored, and emitted by local business be made available to the public and that state and local planning committees be established to create a chemical emergency response plan for every community (Rosenbaum 1991).

While the policies established in RCRA, TSCA, and Superfund identify important contributions in waste control, each suffers procedural limitations in attempting to reconcile waste reduction, control, and cleanup with continued economic expansion. RCRA authorizes the EPA to enforce safe disposal guidelines in those states that fail to do so on their own. But, as in related areas, procedural quagmires have limited success.

Both RCRA and TSCA have experienced repeated delays and setbacks as a result of the breadth of regulations required. The difficulty in obtaining technical data has resulted in a form of administrative overload (Rosenbaum 1991). The EPA has always been underfunded and understaffed for its expanding responsibility, and the lean years between 1980 and 1986 only exacerbated the problems of program management. Moreover, data disclosure was required of chemical producers, but these companies have been traditionally resistant to supplying complete information. By 1985 more than sixty-three thousand chemicals were included on the EPA's chemical inventory (GAO 1986b). The agency simply lacks the resources to verify the information provided. In 1980 then Deputy EPA Administrator John Quarles noted that "in the nine years of EPA's existence, its manpower has roughly doubled while its program responsibilities have multiplied by a factor of 20" (quoted in Mosher 1980:2116). Between 1980 and 1983, in the midst of new waste policy demands, Burford cut the EPA staff by more than one-fifth and cut its non-Superfund budget by almost one-third (Conservation Foundation 1984). By 1988, in spite of major new program responsibilities, the EPA staff was only 3 percent larger than in 1980 (Gruber 1988).

Additionally, staff members have been criticized for conflicts of interest: the first chairman of the agency's Dioxin Implementation Plan was Dr. Ralph Ross, who moved on to the Department of Agriculture from where he lobbied the EPA on behalf of 2,4,5-T, a dioxin-based pesticide. Moreover, there have been serious questions raised about the quality of the agency's scientific research. Dr. Melvin Reuber, who worked for the EPA reviewing safety data on twenty-three registered pesticides, found that a significant portion of the data was inadequate, much of it submitted by manufacturers in the 1950s. Reuber did his own research and found that most of the pesticides were carcinogenic. When he reported the results, EPA officials did nothing, leaving the pesticides registered and available. Reuber charged the agency with generally neglecting its responsibilities:

> Members of the Cancer Assessment Group were not qualified—
> and the work that they turned out was unsatisfactory. Toxicolo-
> gists would do the pathology, anybody would do the
> epidemiology, and there were actually students, high school and
> college students working part-time—who even prepared reports
> for the CAG. (Reuber, quoted in Rabinovitch 1981:261)

Reuber resigned, citing unsatisfactory research and unqualified staff in pathology and epidemiology.

Superfund, even with its increased funding, is recognized to be too little too late. While 1,236 sites are included on the EPA's 1991 National Priority List, the list will likely double as potential sites are evaluated. Further, the number of sites requiring remedial cleanup may exceed 25,000. Yet, since 1980, only 33 sites have been cleaned (Rosenbaum 1991; Viviano 1991). The Office of Technology Assessment estimates that costs of cleaning the priority sites may ultimately exceed $500 billion, significantly more than the $10.1 billion authorized since 1980. Aside from the obvious financial constraints, Superfund has suffered from constant legal battles. Because the act allows the EPA to penalize companies for dumping that was not illegal at the time, legal challenges have been inevitable. Further, corporations have been able to slow implementation to a snail's pace by challenging every administrative step in court (Viviano 1991).

Another major obstacle to cleaning sites is the NIMBY (Not in My Back Yard) syndrome. Success in cleaning waste sites depends on creating safe permanent hazardous waste repositories. But citizens simply do not want hazardous waste brought into their communities. Nimbyism is manifest in community activism, taking advantage of RCRA's and Superfund's provision giving citizens standing to sue federal agencies to enforce federal legislation. Further, the Nuclear Waste Policy Act (NWPA, 1982) requires public hearings in considering potential sites.

To judge the salience of NIMBY consider that in one instance, when the Department of Energy was evaluating sites for a radioactive waste repository, thirty-eight hearings were held in seven states, drawing eighteen thousand people and almost sixty thousand comments (Kraft and Clary 1991). Public opposition is the main obstacle to siting permanent waste facilities, delaying cleanup of several sites.

In 1989, for example, as a result of public concern, Alabama announced that it would no longer accept the annual seven hundred thousand tons of hazardous waste from twenty-two surrounding states (Rosenbaum 1991). Nimbyism is typically an emotional response, with citizens perceiving risks to be higher than scientists admit (Slovic 1987).

But, considering the history of toxic waste management and the general pattern of neglect shown by government agencies involved in toxic cleanups through the 1970s and 1980s, the negative citizen response may indeed be quite rational. Current waste policy all but ignores the reality that citizens do not want waste sites in their communities. The omission is critical, because waste policy is predicated on the notion of safe disposal in appropriate facilities.

Nimbyism itself may be a function of Liberal culture. While citizens are slow to acknowledge a communal interest in safe disposal facilities, self-interest motivates the not-in-my-backyard reaction. Public reaction suggests that source reduction may be a more reliable waste policy. In any event, nimbyism begs the question as to whether citizens are prepared to accept the waste management responsibilities Liberal society creates.

To understand waste policy more effectively, it is useful to explore what federal waste policy fails to do. As mentioned above, the single largest impediment to successful waste management is the lack of resources (funds and staff) authorized by RCRA, TSCA, and Superfund. Equally important, however, is the focus of the legislation. Each seeks to identify and catalogue "waste." Once defined, the various waste is to be "controlled." Rather than reduce waste, the regulations define disposal guidelines. Although RCRA required investigating the viability of recycling and conservation programs, regulators have seen conservation and recycling as local models that have no place in federal policy. Reducing waste, however, is the main ingredient in managing both solid and hazardous waste, as safe disposal is only possible with a manageable amount of waste.

The Clinton-Gore administration has placed conservation at the center of its environmental agenda (Clinton and Gore 1992). But it has yet to explain substantively how it will encourage conservation without restraining economic growth. The Clinton-Gore approach, as outlined during the 1992 campaign, claims to

> shatter the false choice between environmental protection and economic growth by creating a market-based environmental protection strategy that rewards conservation and "green" business practices while penalizing polluters. (Clinton and Gore 1992:94)

This, Clinton and Gore explain, will be done by creating tax incentives that favor the use of recycled materials, thus expanding waste recovery markets. Further, they favor transferring federal Superfund dollars away from litigation and into actual cleanup.

The plans have yet to be explained substantively. While the economic problems Clinton has inherited have clearly taken priority, his ability to balance the consumption and conservation dilemma will determine the success of his waste plans. Clinton and Gore accept the assumptions of liberalism—e.g., individual self-interest is the best way to maximize economic growth—without accepting the implications. Minimizing waste necessitates placing the common good on an equal footing with individual good.

The Clinton-Gore plan notwithstanding, federal policy makers have traditionally been hesitant to approach the waste problem aggressively because they fear that over-regulation will inhibit economic growth. The problem of waste management in Liberal society hinges on the consumption and conservation dilemma. Reducing waste requires recovering and reusing products and resources. This, in effect, will reduce the volume of overall sales of these products and resources, cutting into the profit margins of manufacturers. It is apparent that policy makers will consistently choose economic growth over waste reduction. While policy makers may be truly concerned about growing solid and hazardous waste, the weak model of existing regulations focusing on waste identification, cataloging, and "control" (e.g., "proper disposal") is simply incapable of solving the waste problem.

Conclusion

The Liberal emphasis on economic expansion results in an ever-increasing amount of waste. The constant drive to find new markets for this expanded production encourages the disposability of consumer goods. At the same time, the drive for profit maximization creates an economic incentive for companies to employ the cheapest production and disposal methods, fostering inadequate and unsafe waste management. Waste policy serves to obfuscate the tension by claiming that waste can be controlled simply by regulating disposal. In failing to address the larger question of waste reduction, policy makers are seeking to reassure an anxious public at the expense of confronting the waste problem substantively. In this sense, waste policy is symbolic.

This chapter has argued that, in placing private self-interest above communal good, liberalism is unable to solve the waste dilemma. Further, the chapter argued that existing models of waste management policy are weak and ineffective, ensuring that our current waste problem will continue. The following chapter explores energy policy and the tensions between liberalism and environmental quality in energy production and use.

7 Energy and the Politics of Consumption

The United States currently uses approximately one quarter of the world's energy—24 percent (Energy Information Administration [EIA] 1992). Yet, with that, the United States gets only half as much of the efficiency per unit of energy as western Europe or Japan (World Resources Institute 1993). The average American will use more energy this year than the average resident of Europe, of South America, and of Japan combined (World Resources Institute 1993; Corson 1990).

Energy use is directly tied to environmental quality. In the United States, energy combustion is responsible for 36 percent of particulate matter, 37 percent of hydrocarbons, 83 percent of carbon monoxide, 84 percent of sulfur oxides, and 95 percent of nitrogen oxides in air (Rosenbaum 1991). Additionally, more than 20 million gallons of oil and related chemicals are accidentally spilled in an average year—around ten thousand spills annually in U.S. waters. And almost 6 million acres have been destroyed by coal mining in the United States (Rosenbaum 1991). Further, while it is apparent that there is only a generation left of fossil fuel reserves, the United States has no national energy policy with specific guidelines and long-term goals spelled out.

Energy production and use has not formally been tied to the environmental bureaucracy. The Department of Energy (DOE) has consistently been thought of as a governmental assistant to power companies. It is common for DOE personnel to revolve between private-sector power companies and regulatory responsibility. Hazel O'Leary, Clinton's secretary of energy, illustrates the point. O'Leary was a senior DOE regulator during the Carter administration. Later, with her husband John O'Leary (who ran the Pennsylvania utility that owns the Three Mile Island Plant), she was an independent energy consultant in Washington, D.C. Most recently she was executive vice-president for corporate affairs at Northern States Power Company, one of the largest utilities in the nation. There O'Leary was responsible for lobbying government on behalf of Northern States' corporate interest. It was

O'Leary's awkward responsibility to defend the company when it repeatedly came under fire from regulators over the disposal of its radioactive nuclear waste (Lippman 1993).

The Department of Energy, along with the Department of Defense, has long been one of the nation's worst environmental polluters. The need for an environmentally conscious secretary of energy was underscored in 1988 by the public discovery that the DOE had mismanaged military nuclear reactors and radioactive waste for at least three decades (Rosenbaum 1991:107). As a consequence of the separation between energy and environmental quality, environmental protection through energy conservation has not been a policy priority.

This chapter explores the relationship between energy production and use and environmental degradation. As well, the chapter examines the economic and political constraints to conservation. Ultimately, the chapter argues that the tension between liberalism and environmental policy making is manifest in consumptive energy priorities.

Energy Production and Environmental Quality

The major sources of energy in the United States are fossil fuels—representing 89 percent of all energy consumed (Energy Information Administration [EIA] 1992). Hydroelectric and nuclear, and to a much smaller extent geothermal and biomass, account for the rest. Renewable energy sources such as biomass, wind, geothermal, and solar, while potentially major energy resources are currently without priority. In fact, the Department of Energy's *International Energy Annual*, the main summary of energy resources, does not even mention these sources (EIA 1992).

U.S. energy consumption has steadily increased, peaking in the mid-1980s and declining slightly since. Between 1981 and 1990 U.S. oil, gas, and hydroelectric reliance has declined slightly, while nuclear reliance has more than doubled. Table 7.1 illustrates these trends. Worldwide, reliance on all energy sources has increased. The United States currently imports 17 percent of its energy resources (EIA 1992). Table 7.2 shows the relative importance of each energy source: 41.3 percent of U.S. energy is provided by oil, 23.9 percent by natural gas, 23.5 percent by coal, 3.6 percent by hydroelectric plants, and 7.6 percent by nuclear plants. Worldwide, 39.2 percent of energy comes from oil, 21.4 percent from natural gas, 27.1 percent from coal, 6.4 percent from hydroelectric plants, and 5.9 percent from nuclear plants (EIA 1992).

TABLE 7.1. U.S. and World Energy Consumption, by Source, 1981–1990

United States	1981	1982	1983	1984	1985	1986	1987	1988	1989	1990
Oil[1]	16,058	15,296	15,231	15,726	15,726	16,281	16,665	17,283	17,325	16,988
Gas[2]	19,404	18,001	16,835	17,951	17,281	16,221	17,211	18,030	18,799	18,815
Coal[3]	732.63	706.91	736.67	791.29	818.05	804.31	836.94	883.66	890.56	894.56
Hydro[4]	297.0	341.7	370.6	363.9	325.3	329.9	299.2	257.8	279.2	285.0
Nuclear[4]	272.7	282.8	293.7	327.6	383.7	414.0	455.3	527.0	529.4	576.9
World Total										
Oil[1]	60,866	59,465	58,691	59,784	59,863	61,509	62,773	64,497	65,709	65,901
Gas[2]	53,610	53,069	54,420	59,105	61,999	62,790	65,910	69,366	72,270	74,423
Coal[3]	4,219.2	4,324.3	4,358.3	4,492.2	4,783.0	4,893.1	4,994.8	5,117.1	5,272.3	5,171.2
Hydro[4]	1,766.2	1,812.1	1,903.9	1,960.7	1,979.2	2,018.9	2,028.4	2,076.6	2,056.3	2,112.9
Nuclear[4]	778.7	866.5	981.8	1,197.0	1,425.7	1,517.7	1,654.0	1,794.8	1,843.3	1,898.3

[1]Thousand Barrels per Day

[2]Billion Cubic Feet

[3]Million Short Tons

[4]Billion Kilowatthours

Source: Energy Information Administration, 1992, *International Energy Annual, 1990* (Washington, DC: Department of Energy).

TABLE 7.2. Total U.S. and World Energy Production and Consumption, 1990 (in Quadrillion [10^{15}] Btu)

	Oil	Gas[1]	Gas[2]	Coal	Hydro	Nuclear	Total
United States Production	15.27	2.17	18.15	22.46	2.92	6.19	67.47
United States Consumption	33.55		19.40	19.09	2.94	6.19	81.17
Percent of Total 1990 Energy Consumption	41.3		23.9	23.5	3.6	7.6	
World Production	129.06	7.19	73.50	93.00	21.95	20.35	345.06
World Consumption	135.01		73.70	93.20	21.96	20.35	344.21
Percent of Total 1990 Energy Consumption	39.2		21.4	27.1	6.4	5.9	

[1]Natural Gas Plant Liquids

[2]Dry Natural Gas

Source: Energy Information Administration, 1992, *International Energy Annual, 1990* (Washington, DC: Department of Energy).

Oil

Petroleum is clearly the single most important energy resource, both in the United States and worldwide. Yet, according to the U.S. Department of Energy, at the rate of current consumption, known world oil reserves will be depleted by 2032 (EIA 1992). While the United States currently uses almost 25 percent of the world's oil, the United States only holds 3 percent of known reserves. Sixty-two percent of known petroleum reserves are located in the Middle East, with 22 percent in North America, Europe, and Asia combined. The United States currently imports 41 percent of its oil (Oil and Gas Journal 1990).

Oil, like all fossil fuels, presents a particular danger to environmental quality. The burning of petroleum products releases sulfur and nitrogen oxides, carbon monoxide, volatile organic compounds (hydrocarbons), and ozone-causing chemicals. Sulfur and nitrogen oxides are known to damage lungs and other mucous membranes, in addition to being the prime cause of acid precipitation. Carbon monoxide displaces oxygen in red blood cells, damaging the cardiovascular and nervous systems. Additionally, carbon monoxide is a prime contributor to the greenhouse effect. Hydrocarbons are thought to be carcinogenic, and VOCs contribute to ozone smog. Ozone, created by the atmospheric reaction between nitrogen oxides and VOCs in sunlight, causes eye and mucous membrane irritation and reduced lung capacity and contributes to asthma and other respiratory problems. Ozone also injures trees, crops, and other plants, and contributes to global warming (Corson 1990).

Natural Gas

Natural gas is the second major source of U.S. energy, accounting for 24 percent of energy used (EIA 1992). At the current rate of consumption, known world gas reserves will be depleted by 2048 (EIA 1992; *World Oil* 1991; *Oil and Gas Journal* 1990). And, as with petroleum, while the United States uses one-quarter of the world's gas, only 4 percent of total known gas reserves are within the United States (*World Oil* 1991). Known natural gas reserves are concentrated in eastern Europe (37 percent) and the Middle East (31 percent). North America holds 8 percent of the known reserves, western Europe holds 5 percent, and Asia holds 8 percent (*Oil and Gas Journal* 1990; *World Oil* 1991).

Natural gas is the cleanest fossil fuel, emitting 80 percent less carbon dioxide than coal (Corson 1990). Nonetheless, natural gas does release significant amounts of all fossil related emissions. While burning cleaner than either oil or coal, natural gas does contribute to air pollution and global warming.

Coal

Coal accounts for 24 percent of U.S. energy needs (EIA 1992). Coal is the only fuel that the United States consumed at a rate lower than its production in 1990 (EIA 1992). The United States consumes 17 percent of the world's coal, while holding 23 percent of known recoverable world reserves. At current consumption rates, recoverable world coal reserves will last to 2336, the longest of the fossil fuels (World Energy Council 1989; British Petroleum 1991; EIA 1992). This, of course, does not account for a greater reliance on coal as other resources become depleted. Air pollution concerns aside, if coal use were to replace depleted oil and natural gas reserves, coal reserves would be depleted by 2100 (EIA 1992).

Coal is the dirtiest fossil fuel. Even with improved "clean" technologies, coal emits 25 percent more carbon dioxide than oil, and 80 percent more CO_2 than natural gas (Corson 1990). In Czechoslovakia, coal related air pollution is so severe respiratory infections are commonplace, and crop damage is extensive. Czech scientists estimate air-pollution-related crop damage at $192 million annually (Corson 1990; Brown 1993). Coal emissions present a significant threat to public health and are primary contributors to acid rain and global warming.

Hydroelectric Power

Water-powered generators produce 3.6 percent of total United States energy (EIA 1992). Hydropower is considered renewable and clean in that water is a constant resource in many areas and hydroelectric plants produce no waste. However, hydroelectric plants have a significant impact on local ecosystems. Hydroelectric dams are responsible for flooding sensitive valleys, such as Yosemite's Hetch Hetchy valley. The damming of rivers has permanently blocked freshwater fish, such as salmon, from access to spawning regions. Flooded spawning beds and warmer water temperatures caused by slowed water movement inhibit spawning even further. And, the diversion of water creates both flooded canyons in some areas and low water levels in others.

The Nuclear Option

Nuclear power provides 7.5 percent of U.S. energy needs (EIA 1992). While production of all other energy sources has remained relatively stagnant in recent years, nuclear production has doubled since 1981 (see Table 7.1; EIA 1992). The United States alone produces and consumes 30 percent of the globe's nuclear energy (EIA 1992). In 1993, there were 109 licensed nuclear power plants in the United States, down from 112 in 1990 (NRC 1993; Rosenbaum 1991). Atomic power has sustained the dreams of energy security since its origins in the military in the 1930s. It is, therefore, appropriate to explore the nuclear option in greater detail.

Nuclear energy presents special problems for environmental quality. While proponents of nuclear power consistently remind the public that nuclear plants release no emissions, the energy used in the mining and preparation of uranium releases significant amounts of carbon dioxide (Corson 1990). And, perhaps more important, the production of nuclear power creates a vast amount of radioactive waste. Furthermore, nuclear reactors have a limited life, and then must be dismantled, a process that itself presents dilemmas. And, the history of accidents at nuclear plants, both within the United States and abroad, suggests that the nuclear option may, in the long run, be quite dangerous.

A typical commercial reactor produces about 30 metric tons of spent radioactive fuel every year. By 1990, the accumulation of irradiated fuel from commercial nuclear plants in the United States had reached 21,800 metric tons and is expected to reach 40,400 metric tons by 2000. At discharge, each ton of nuclear waste emits 177,242,000 curies—or about as much radiation as 177 Hiroshima and Nagasaki atom bombs. This radioactivity takes several thousand generations to decay. Plutonium-239, for example, has a half-life (the time it takes for half of the original radioactivity to decay) of 24,400 years, posing serious dangers for about 250,000 years (Brown 1992).

Safe storage of these radioactive wastes is the major issue. Currently, more than 100 million gallons of high level liquid waste is temporarily stored at facilities in Washington, Idaho, South Carolina, and New York. Another six thousand metric tons of spent fuel is stored in cooling ponds at nuclear plants. This is expected to reach sixty-three thousand metric tons by 1995 (Rosenbaum 1991). Accidental spills and seepage into groundwater is not uncommon, particularly at nuclear weapons facilities. In the late 1980s the DOE revealed mismanagement and deliberate suppression of information about accidents at all of its nuclear facilities (Rosenbaum 1991). The *New York Times* revealed that the Atomic Energy Commission had suppressed major accidents at nuclear facilities during the 1950s and 1960s (*New York Times* 1988c; *New York Times* 1989a; *New York Times* 1989b). Similarly, the DOE revealed that radioactive wastes had been leaking from temporary containment structures at nuclear facilities in Rocky Flats, Colorado, and Fernald, Ohio (Rosenbaum 1991). Permanent storage continues to be a contentious issue in policy circles. In 1989 the DOE announced that the creation of a safe waste repository would be delayed until at least 2010 (Rosenbaum 1991). Yet even this late date may be a pipe dream since there is currently no technology available for safe permanent disposal (Brown 1992).

Nuclear reactors have a limited life-span, typically between thirty and forty years (Davis 1993). Of the 109 plants currently operating, half will be retired by 2015, with all current plants being retired by 2075 (NRC 1993; Rosenbaum 1991). Decommissioning nuclear reactors involves the removal and disposal of all radioactive materials—spent fuel, soil, ground water, buildings, and equipment. No major commercial reactors have been decommissioned yet, but the costs of decommissioning a single reactor are expected to range from 50 million to over 3 billion dollars (Davis 1993; Rosenbaum 1991). Further, the decommissioning of reactors assumes there will be safe permanent disposal sites.

The safety of nuclear power is based on safe disposal and prevention of accidents. Safe disposal technologies do not yet exist. And, several serious accidents place doubt on the long-term viability of safely operating nuclear plants. Several major accidents occurred at nuclear facilities during the 1950s and 1960s (*New York Times* 1988c; *New York*

Times 1989a; *New York Times* 1989b). Serious accidents have occurred throughout the world, most notably Kyshtym (1957), in the Soviet Union, Windscale (1957), England, Three Mile Island (1979), United States, and Chernobyl (1986), Soviet Union.

At Three Mile Island, a faulty pump and operator error resulted in the draining of cooling water from the reactor core, allowing the temperature to rise above five thousand degrees Fahrenheit. The reactor's containment system came dangerously close to releasing an estimated 18 billion curies of radiation—more than one hundred times that released in Chernobyl (Corson 1990). As late as 1989, only 20 percent of nuclear utilities had completed safety changes instituted by the Nuclear Regulatory Commission following Three Mile Island in 1979 (Rosenbaum 1991). Accidents at nuclear power plants are more common than the public realizes. In 1987 alone, there were nearly 3000 reported minor accidents, 430 emergency shutdowns, and nearly 104,000 incidents of accidental exposure to measurable doses of radiation (Corson 1990).

The combined costs of building facilities, disposing of radioactive wastes, decommissioning reactors, and cleaning up accidents have made it increasingly clear that economically nuclear power may be a poor option. The construction and startup costs of the Seabrook nuclear power plant in New Hampshire exceeded $5.8 billion, more than six times the expected cost of $900 million (Rosenbaum 1991). Disposal costs are similarly astronomic. The cost of a ninety-six thousand-ton capacity burial site is expected to exceed $36 billion (Brown 1992). Reactor decommissioning is expected to cost several hundred million dollars for each facility (Rosenbaum 1991). And, finally, cleanup costs of actual and potential accidents will come to billions of dollars. The Three Mile Island cleanup has exceeded $1 billion, while the damage caused at Chernobyl has been estimated at $10 billion (Corson 1990).

The future of nuclear energy remains uncertain. The problems of high cost, waste disposal, perceived safety risks, and the growing public pressure against siting plants and waste facilities has made nuclear power increasingly problematic—as the dropping number of operating plants and the cancellations of new projects suggests. Still, energy analysts argue that these problems can be resolved and that nuclear power remains a viable alternative (Davis 1993).

The Energy Dilemma

Clearly, there is an energy dilemma in the United States. At current consumption rates the United States, like the rest of the world, will have depleted traditional energy resources within a generation. The production

of nuclear power is not yet safe or affordable. Yet there appears to be little concern expressed either by governments or by citizens. There is an
apparent assumption that as resources are depleted new energy resources will replace them and new technologies will be developed that
will enable different energy sources to be utilized. In the end, either of
these may occur. But a nagging question must be addressed: Why are
we as a society moving toward the future as if we had unlimited supplies of safe energy resources? Conversely, if we as a society, by necessity, must eventually develop renewable, clean, and safe energy
resources, why are we waiting until we deplete existing resources and
degrade the environment even further? These are not easy questions to
answer, but the legacy of liberalism may offer some insights. The following section explores these issues explicitly.

The Tension between Liberalism and Conservation: The Politics of Consumption

American society grew up with the security of abundant natural resources—land, water, vast forests, oil, natural gas, and coal (Rosenbaum 1991). The vast American West, from Kentucky to California, was
conquered and settled on the promise of unlimited land and materials.
Therefore, forests could be cleared, water diverted and polluted,
prairies overgrazed, and mountains strip-mined with little concern. As
resources were depleted, the nation would simply look west for more.
The Liberal ethic of mixing labor with nature to create value flourished
in the unequaled expanse of American wilderness. Throughout the
eighteenth and nineteenth centuries these resources appeared to most
as though they would last forever.

The adolescent American psyche—itself a product of Lockean liberalism—came of age during the expansionary 1800s. The character of
the nation was deeply imprinted by the assumption of infinite resources. American resource and energy policy, as a consequence, has
traditionally been based on expanding production ("growing the economy") to allow increased consumption. And that—the American emphasis on consumption—is the problem.

It has become increasingly clear since the beginning of this century
that resources are indeed limited. Nonetheless, conservation has been
extraordinarily difficult for Americans. The material needs of the second world war imposed the necessity of rationing, equating conservation with patriotism and national service. But, failing that type of crisis,
Americans have been virtually unwilling to reduce consumption. Per

capita energy consumption has consistently been increasing, peaking in 1980 and dropping slightly since (see Table 7.3).

It wasn't until the 1973 to 1978 energy crisis that a conservational ethic appeared, albeit in embryonic form. The phrase "crisis" itself suggests a sudden and decisive event. In reality, the energy crisis of the 1970s was anything but sudden. In 1973 the United States imported 38.8 percent of its oil (Rosenbaum 1991). The vulnerability of the United States to energy-exporting nations was clear long before the "crisis" hit. Nonetheless, when Arab nations briefly stopped shipping oil in response to U.S. support of Israel in the 1973 Yom Kippur war, the United States went into an energy panic. The United States was forced to recognize its dependence on foreign oil and the vulnerability that dependence engendered. But by the early 1980s the concern dissipated. The lesson did not last long. By 1990 the United States consumed 55 percent more oil than it produced (EIA 1992).

The United States lags far behind most other industrial democracies in energy efficiency. As Table 7.4 illustrates, U.S. per capita energy consumption is greater than that of every nation except Canada and Norway. When efficiency is measured as the ratio of per capita GNP to per capita BTUs, the United States gets approximately one-third the efficiency of Switzerland and Japan, and about one-half the efficiency of western Europe (World Resources Institute 1993). Specifically, for every million BTUs used in Switzerland or Japan, $181 of GNP is created; for every million BTUs used in the United States, $68 of GNP is created (Table 7.4). This lack of efficiency is related both to the Liberal ethic of

TABLE 7.3. U.S. Energy Consumption, 1950–1990

Year:	Per Capita Energy Consumption (million btu):
1950	219
1955	235
1960	244
1965	272
1970	327
1975	327
1980	335
1985	310
1990	309

Sources: Energy Information Administration, 1991, *International Energy Annual, 1990* (Washington, DC: Department of Energy); Council on Environmental Quality, 1992, *Environmental Quality Twenty-Second Annual Report* (Washington, DC: GPO); World Resources Institute, 1993, *The 1993 Information Please Environmental Almanac* (New York: Houghton Mifflin, 1993).

TABLE 7.4. Energy Efficiency of Selected Countries, 1992 (In Descending Order)

Country	Per Capita Energy Consumption (million btu)	Per Capita by GNP (1992 dollars)	Efficiency[1] As Measured 1992 dollars per million btu
Switzerland	177	28,019	180.77
Japan	128	23,072	180.25
Denmark	138	19,535	141.56
Italy	115	15,033	130.72
Israel	84	9,922	118.12
Spain	82	9,626	117.39
France	149	17,052	114.44
Germany (united)	179	19,633	109.68
Finland	222	22,770	102.57
United Kingdom	150	14,669	97.70
Sweden	266	21,958	82.55
Netherlands	189	14,878	78.72
United States	**309**	**21,039**	**68.08**
Iceland	282	18,710	66.35
Brazil	47	2,952	62.81
Norway	370	22,005	59.47
Canada	400	20,224	50.56
Mexico	52	2,332	44.85
Saudi Arabia	177	6,319	35.70
India	12	314	26.17
Venezuela	92	2,156	23.43
China	24	374	15.58

[1]This index is based on the ratio between per capita GNP and per capita energy consumption. Efficiency is calculated by dividing the per capita GNP dollars (1992) by the per capita energy consumption (1992).

Source: Calculated from data provided by World Resources Institute, 1993, *The 1993 Information Please Environmental Almanac* (New York: Houghton Mifflin)

consumption and to the recognition that the United States, unlike most nations, has the capacity and the will to use its military to ensure a cheap and abundant supply of energy fuels. The Persian Gulf War is only one recent example of U.S. resolve to ensure viable energy markets.

When the question above—why is the nation moving toward certain depletion of scarce energy resources with little apparent concern?—is considered in the context of American liberalism, two issues become apparent. First, as a consequence of the American obsession with consumption, the United States has a long history of overusing resources before instituting conservational limits. The destruction of wetlands and wilderness areas, the continuing havoc wrought by strip-mining, the degradation of surface waters and aquifers, the poisoning of coastal regions with oil drilling and sewage dumping, and the destruction of the few remaining old growth forest areas all suggest that energy resources will be virtually used up—the environmental impact notwithstanding—before serious efforts at developing renewable, safe, and clean energy sources occurs. Second, traditional energy sources such as fossil fuels and nuclear power are deeply entrenched in the current economy. The transition from traditional to renewable energy sources will be costly to certain industries. In particular, this transition threatens the economic hegemony of traditional utilities and oil companies.

As Chapter 1 discussed, economic success in the United States has historically been defined by economic growth. To maximize individual and corporate profit, and to minimize recessionary contractions, American capitalism has relied on continual economic expansion. While one would expect the GNP to grow consistently with the growth of population, the drive to maximize profits pushes greater efficiency from industrial processes and expansion of markets to maximize productivity. As a consequence, production has required ever greater amounts of energy. As Table 7.5 illustrates, while population in the United States grew by 39 percent between 1960 and 1990, GNP rose by 150 percent. This greater productivity came as a result of new technologies that made manufacturing more efficient and production materials cheaper. But this was not without a cost. During the same time, energy consumption increased by 85 percent (see Table 7.5).

Oil and natural gas continue to be the cheapest fuel, especially considering the subsidies provided by the U.S. Department of Energy and the armed forces. Federal funding of fossil fuel energy research in 1990 was five times greater than research for renewable energy sources, approximately $650 million to $132 million (Holdren 1991). Further, the Defense Department subsidizes the oil industry by ensuring access to overseas petroleum. The Gulf War was clearly fought to secure oil reserves in Kuwait, Saudi Arabia, and the United Arab Emirates at a cost of over $100 billion (Mandel 1991). In addition, the nuclear industry receives direct governmental subsidies totaling between $12 billion and $15 billion annually and several indirect subsidies such as the Price-Anderson Act (1957) which limits a nuclear utility's liability to $540 million for any accident (Rosenbaum 1991). There is, consequently, little incentive for conservation or transition to renewable energy technologies.

While the DOE estimates that there are sufficient renewable energy sources to provide for 50 to 70 percent of current energy needs by 2030, U.S. funding of these technologies has been cut by 80 percent since

TABLE 7.5. U.S. Population Growth, GNP Growth, and Energy Consumption, 1960–1990

Year	Population (millions)	GNP (billions of 1982 dollars)	Total U.S. Energy Consumption (quadrillion btu)
1960	180.7	1,665.3	43.8
1965	194.3	2,087.6	52.7
1970	205.1	2,416.2	66.4
1975	216.0	2,695.0	70.6
1980	227.7	3,187.1	76.0
1985	238.5	3,618.7	73.9
1990	250.0	4,155.8	81.2

Percent Increase:

Year	Population	GNP	Energy
1960–70	13.5	45	52
1970–80	11.0	32	15
1980–90	10.0	30	7
1960–90	39.0	150	85

Sources: U.S. Department of Commerce, Bureau of the Census, 1991, *Current Population Reports* (Washington, DC: GPO); Executive Office of the President, Council of Economic Advisors, 1991, *1991 Economic Report* Washington, DC: GPO); U.S. Department of Energy, Energy Information Administration, 1990, *Annual Energy Outlook 1990 with Projections to 2010* (Washington, DC: GPO); U.S. Department of Energy, Energy Information Administration, 1992, *International Energy Annual 1990* (Washington, DC: GPO).

1980 (Brown, et al., 1991; Corson 1990). The traditional energy policies of subsidizing fossil fuel and nuclear power has not solved the problems of environmental degradation or energy dependency. It is clear that alternative energy resources will have to be developed within the next generation. There are already several viable technologies which may provide clean and renewable energy. These technologies are addressed later in the chapter.

Energy Policy and Symbolic Politics: The Growth/ Conservation Dilemma

American energy policy has traditionally been market driven (Smith 1992). That is, profit maximization has typically driven energy exploration and development. As a consequence, increased consumption has been a fundamental aspect of U.S. energy policy. American political culture, reflecting its Lockean heritage, has consistently defined the main role of government in economic terms: protecting private property and maximizing economic growth. The consequence, as we have seen, is consumption-driven energy policies with severe environmental degradation as a byproduct.

If energy policy is driven by market incentives, the need for solving immediate crises outweighs the need for long-term planning (Smith 1992). As chapters 1 and 2 point out, policy makers are extraordinarily sensitive to maximizing economic growth. As a consequence, short-term economic concerns often take precedence over long-term resource management. This is the dilemma for policy makers. Prudent energy planning necessitates conserving energy resources (conservation); maximizing market expansion necessitates cheap and abundant fuels (consumption).

Evolving Energy Policy: Coal, Oil, and Gas

The vast American wilderness was conquered and settled on the promise of unlimited land and materials. As resources were depleted the nation would simply look west for more. Throughout the eighteenth and nineteenth centuries these resources appeared to most as though they would last forever. As a result, American resource and energy policy has traditionally been based on expanding production to allow increased consumption.

Coal was the first energy source to fuel the industrial revolution. It burns far more efficiently than wood, requires no processing, and can be used as a mobile fuel source. By 1880 coal accounted for 90 percent of locomotive fuel and was a significant source of fuel for steam-operated machinery (Smith 1992). Coal use has largely remained unregulated, though there are a few significant policies affecting mining and burning.

The 1970 Clean Air Act amendments restricted some coal burning in an effort to reduce sulfur oxide emissions. Later, in the face of the "energy crisis" the Energy Supply and Environmental Coordination Act of 1974 provided waivers to certain Clean Air Act requirements in an effort to increase the use of coal. By 1977, in the face of new economic and energy concerns, Congress extended for two more years all emission deadlines, which were to be followed by tighter hydrocarbon and nitrogen oxide standards (Clean Air Act amendments of 1977).

The Surface Mining Control and Reclamation Act (SMCRA 1977) established limits on mining on farmlands, alluvial valleys, and slopes (Vig and Kraft 1990). Further, SMCRA requires that mined land be restored to its original contours. The 1990 Clean Air Act amendments further restricted the use of coal. Other regulations on coal have typically focused on mining safety issues (Davis 1993).

Oil came to dominate energy politics during the 1920s. Oil was a critical fuel in both World Wars, powering the massive U.S. Navy, transporting ground troops and fueling armored divisions and air support. Oil made possible the country's vast domestic economic infrastructure. The industrial boom in the 1920s was a direct consequence of petroleum-based fuels, including electricity. Transportation—both of people and of products—came to rely on ship oil, diesel fuel, gasoline, and later jet fuel. It is not surprising that national security, both military and economic, has come to rely on cheap and abundant oil.

Like coal, oil development and distribution originated in private corporations. The relatively large capital investment required to drill and process petroleum products resulted in a small number of corporations dominating the industry. Curiously, it was antitrust laws that first came to regulate the oil industry. In 1911 the Supreme Court split the Standard Oil Company into successor companies. Of the seven largest oil companies in operation today, five—Exxon, Mobil, Chevron, Amoco, and BP/Sohio—are direct heirs of the original Standard Oil (Davis 1993).

By the 1970s, regulations affecting petroleum products became increasingly salient, both due to environmental issues (e.g., air pollution and oil spills) and to perceptions of inadequate energy supplies. The 1970 Clean Air Act amendments regulated emissions from internal combustion engines (both diesel and gasoline). A series of laws— Nixon's wage-price freeze in 1977, the Emergency Petroleum Allocation Act (1973), and the Energy Policy and Conservation Act (1975)—established price ceilings on oil in an effort to stabilize petroleum prices.

As a result of the Arab Oil Embargo and the public concern that ensued, every president since Nixon has called for a substantial increase in coal consumption to reduce U.S. reliance on imported oil. Further, Ford and Carter both sought conservation as a necessary component of energy independence, suggesting that the traditional Liberal anticonservation ethic was beginning to crack—at least until 1980 and the election of Ronald Reagan.

In 1975 Congress established auto efficiency standards. The standards successfully raised auto efficiency from an average 14.2 miles per gallon (mpg) in 1974 to 28.5 in 1988 (Rosenbaum 1991). By 1975 Ford signed the Strategic Petroleum Reserve (SPR) into law. The SPR set aside 500 million barrels of oil in underground storage in Louisiana and Texas (Davis 1993). The reserve was intended to offset shortages caused by national emergencies or boycotts.

The 1990 Clean Air Act amendments mandated a variety of pollution controls that affect oil. These include reformulating motor fuels in nonattainment areas, increased vehicle mileage standards, and the development of nonpetroleum-based and hybrid fuels to offset heavy petroleum consumption. Further, the amendments restate standards and deadlines for meeting National Ambient Air Quality Standards (NAAQS). This will require regional action to minimize petroleum consumption.

Natural gas arrived on the energy scene in the 1920s as a byproduct of oil exploration. Unlike coal or oil, gas initially had few uses because of its difficult transportation and storage requirements and was simply burned off at its source. Gas use required vast pipeline networks to distribute it from its sources to its users. As advances in welding allowed improved pipeline construction in the 1930s gas became a common energy source.

The reliance on pipeline systems made gas companies natural monopolies—consumers had to purchase gas from the company that delivered it to their door (Davis 1993). Thus, conventional antitrust regulations could not apply to gas distributors. Vast holding companies emerged. In 1935 the Public Utility Holding Company Act placed regulatory control of these companies in the Securities and Exchange Commission (SEC). Through the Holding Company Act, the SEC created geographically defined regional utilities.

The Natural Gas Act (1938) placed regulation of interstate gas movement in the Federal Power Commission (later becoming the Federal Energy Regulatory Commission), which had already been overseeing electrical utilities. The FPC was responsible for issuing permits for new pipeline construction and for expansion of gas facilities. By 1954, the Supreme Court gave the FPC the right to regulate gas prices through *Phillips v. Wisconsin.* This remained in effect until Reagan deregulated utilities in 1985 (Davis 1993).

The Clean Air Act amendments between 1970 and 1990 all encouraged greater usage of natural gas because of its clean burning character. The 1990 amendments, in particular, require the EPA to issue regulations requiring commercial fleets of ten or more (excluding emergency vehicles) capable of being centrally fueled to use "clean fuels"—such as methanol, ethanol, propane, or natural gas.

The evolving energy policy bureaucracy has focused primarily on regulating ownership, pricing, fuel distribution networks, worker health and safety, and indirectly, emissions. Yet even with this network of energy policies, the United States still has no overall national energy policy with specific guidelines and long-term goals spelled out.[1]

The sections below explore the evolution of contemporary energy policies. In reviewing the Carter, Reagan, Bush, and Clinton administrations it is possible to identify current energy trends. As the section suggests, the lack of a meaningful national energy policy maintains traditional tensions between liberalism and environmental quality.

The Carter Years

Carter's energy plan reflected traditional concerns. To maximize U.S. energy resources Carter ordered utilities to burn coal—the dirtiest, albeit most plentiful, fuel—in place of oil or gas, and he sought a "streamlined" permit process for nuclear power plants (Rosenbaum 1991). Carter recognized that cheap and abundant energy resources are fundamental requirements for rapid economic expansion.

Carter's synthetic fuel program may best reflect the dilemma. In an effort to minimize dependence on foreign oil and to develop renewable energy resources, Carter pushed for the development of a commercial synthetic fuel industry. The program, passed by Congress in 1980, failed to consider the environmental impact of the industry's highly toxic byproducts (Rosenbaum 1991).

Carter recognized the trade-off: the increased energy independence offered by a greater reliance on coal and synthetic fuels came at the cost of greater environmental degradation. Still, in contrast to previous administrations, conservation and increased energy efficiency were a major part of the Carter energy plan. Carter sought a gas tax as well as a tax on "gas-guzzling" cars. Further, he enforced a fifty-five mile per hour speed limit and efficiency standards on cars and appliances (Davis 1993).

Reagan

Reagan's election brought U.S. energy policy back to the dark ages. Reagan's politics of nostalgia was based largely on the myth that everything in America was great. Conservation, consequently, was not only unnecessary, it was antigrowth, and thus to a symbolic extent anti-American. Reagan froze the mandatory fleet efficiency standards at the 1986 level. As a result, mileage efficiency in new cars actually declined by 4 percent between 1988 and 1990 (Rosenbaum 1991).

Additionally, the raising of national speed limits from fifty-five to sixty-five mph consumed an additional five hundred thousand barrels of oil daily (Rosenbaum 1991). Renewable energy research and development was cut by more than 80 percent from its 1980 level (Corson

1990; Rosenbaum 1991). Federal tax energy credits for wind and solar energy use were abolished.

The Reagan administration deregulated oil and gas prices and sought a massive increase in the leasing of public lands for energy exploration, including sensitive coastal areas, and an attempt at national parklands. Further, the Reagan administration pushed hard for increased nuclear power development, doubling U.S. nuclear capacity from 1980 to 1988 (EIA 1992).

The Reagan energy policy was essentially nonpolicy. The gains in renewable energy technologies and conservation made during the Nixon, Ford, and Carter years were lost. Instead, the Reagan years were characterized by a return to a traditional market-based energy policy and a reliance on fossil fuel exploration—coal and oil in particular—and nuclear power.

Bush

The Bush years were no different. It wasn't until Iraq invaded Kuwait in August 1990 that Bush became concerned with a national energy policy. U.S. oil interests in the region culminated with an American lead invasion the following winter. After several months, the Bush administration presented its post-Gulf energy policy. Not surprisingly, it was based on increasing oil production by opening up the Alaskan National Wildlife Refuge and Arctic Coastal Plain to energy exploration. Conservation was explicitly put aside.

Clinton

The Clinton administration faces a difficult challenge. Clinton was elected in the midst of the worst recession since World War II. As a consequence, economic expansion is his first priority. Yet environmental quality remains a salient issue within the constituency that elected him. While Reagan, and later Bush, could marginalize environmental concerns without alienating their core supporters, Clinton has much less flexibility. During the 1992 campaign Clinton outlined a plan to increase energy efficiency and conservation. It calls for an increase in the corporate average fuel economy standards (CAFE standards) from the current 27.5 mpg to 40 mpg, it encourages mass transit, and it encourages higher efficiency in building materials and appliances (Clinton and Gore 1992).

In his first year as president Clinton made little progress toward a unique energy policy. His most important contribution, the BTU tax (a tax on energy consumption as measured by each British Thermal Unit), was rejected by Congress. A tax on energy consumption would have encouraged energy conservation. Beyond the BTU tax, Clinton has offered little. Clinton was able to get a 4.3-cent-per-gallon increase in the gasoline tax through Congress, but such a marginal tax will not encourage conservation. Even Ronald Reagan signed a five-cent-per-gallon gas tax increase. Clinton constantly refers to "growing the economy," with little explanation of the energy or environmental impact. Furthermore, while Clinton took pains to appoint environmentally friendly administrators to the EPA (Browner) and the Department of Interior (Babbitt), the appointment of O'Leary to head the DOE shows less concern.

Clinton may mirror the Carter model. Even though he may be genuinely concerned about environmental quality, the short-term constraints of economic expansion and assuring abundant cheap energy may result in an energy policy that is little different from its predecessors. This may explain why Clinton considers the DOE secretary a part of his economic team rather than his environmental team (Lippman 1993).

Energy Policy and Symbolic Politics

Energy policy has traditionally been problematic in several ways. In placing consumption over conservation, policy makers have encouraged the deeply rooted myth that energy resources are unlimited. Further, the environmental impact of energy production and use has consistently been ignored. When policy makers consciously ignore the larger implications of wasteful consumption and environmental degradation, they are making a symbolic accommodation to the tensions between liberalism and resource management. The lack of concern expressed by citizens is a result of the success of policy makers to divert attention away from long-term problems. Further, the assumption that depleted resources will be replaced by new discoveries is based on our cultural mythology: specifically, that technology will rescue us.

The need for clean renewable energies is clear to those who study aggregate fuel reserves. Nonetheless, policy elites are slow to make the development of these technologies part of their agendas. In the end, traditional energy resources will be depleted and alternatives will be developed. But, if this transition comes as a consequence of market incentive rather than rational long-term planning, we are likely to further degrade the environment in significant ways, particularly in fragile coastal and wilderness areas.

Traditional energy companies, and the industries that rely upon them, will continue to seek the cheapest energy resources available.

And, since profit maximization has no calculation for ecological damage, it is likely that energy exploration will inflict irreversible damage on the few pristine ecosystems left. And, perhaps most disturbing, since this discourse is complex, it holds little salience among the public. Policy makers are therefore free to market their energy policies without concern for improving, or even sustaining, environmental quality.

Alternative Energies

Renewable energy technologies would provide an alternative to the petroleum-based energy dilemma discussed above. Geothermal utilities, alcohol vehicle fuels, and waste to energy facilities are already operating on a limited scale throughout the world. Further developing these technologies will allow a shift away from fossil fuel and nuclear dependency, reducing U.S. reliance on foreign energy supplies and providing a cleaner environment. (WRI and IIED 1987, 1989)

Biomass

Biomass, fuels derived from animal and plant matter, is the oldest energy source. Fuel wood, plants, garbage, and animal waste continue to be major energy resources, providing up to 90 percent of energy in many nonindustrial nations (Corson 1990). Over the past twenty years, new technologies have allowed the development of substantially cleaner burning biomass fuels. Alcohol-based fuels, including ethanol (ethyl alcohol), methanol (ethanol and methane), and gasohol (gasoline and ethanol), offer renewable fuels that burn cleaner than conventional gasoline and diesel. Ethanol, produced from any number of crops, including sugarcane, corn, wood, and organic solid waste, has a high oxygen content, allowing more efficient combustion. Alcohol-burning vehicles emit little or no nitrogen oxides or hydrocarbons, reducing ozone smog.

Organic wastes, including biodegradable solid waste, animal waste, plants, and municipal solid wastes can be processed to produce methane, a renewable natural gas. Biomass fuels are particularly important because they can be used to replace traditional petroleum-based mobile fuels, such as gasoline. In Brazil, one-half of automotive fuel is derived from sugarcane (Corson 1990). Still, biomass fuels are no panacea. Low-tech fuels—such as wood—are much dirtier than existing fuels. Additionally, even distilled biomass fuels release carbon dioxide, albeit at lower levels than traditional fossil fuels. Further, diversion of crop residues from fertilization to fuel can reduce soil fertility.

Wind

Wind is one of the oldest energy resources, directly fueling world trade until as late as the first world war. The harnessing of wind power has propelled ships and pumped water for thousands of years. The contemporary use of wind utilizes similar technologies. By 1991, wind turbines worldwide produced 2,215 megawatts of power, an output equal to two large nuclear power plants (Brown, Flavin, and Kane 1992).

Wind farms have appeared in several states around the United States, including California, Vermont, Hawaii, Oregon, Massachusetts, New York, and Montana (Smith 1992). California leads the nation in wind power, producing sixteen hundred megawatts with fifteen thousand turbines located in three farms—the Altamont Pass east of San Francisco, the San Gorgonio Pass east of Los Angeles, and the Tehachapi Mountains north of Los Angeles (Brown, Flavin, and Kane 1992). Wind farms would provide an even greater share of U.S. energy needs if the tax credit for wind energy had not been eliminated in 1985. It is estimated that 25 percent of the nation's electrical needs can be met by installing wind turbines on the windiest 1.5 percent of land (Brown, Flavin, and Kane 1992).

Although the cost of harnessing wind power is comparable to traditional sources (Smith 1992), there are problems. Wind is not constant, and consequently wind power must be supplemented with other sources. Additionally, many of the best locations are already occupied, and turbines may interfere with electronic media transmissions and migratory birds (Smith 1992). Further, large wind farms can ruin the aesthetic value of pristine open space areas.

Solar: Thermal

The sun is the source of all energy on earth. Photosynthesis allows plant and animal life to exist. Wind is caused by thermal differences throughout the planet. The sun illuminates the earth and provides necessary warmth. But, in addition to the passive thermal energy that has allowed for life on the planet, solar energy may provide an answer to our current energy needs.

Solar energy can be used to heat water and buildings or to generate electricity. In Israel, 65 percent of houses have solar water heaters. In Cypress, 90 percent have solar water heating. In the United States solar water systems were becoming increasingly popular, but the elimination of energy tax credits in the mid-1980s, combined with lower oil and gas prices, decimated the industry (Corson 1990).

Complex refractive solar energy systems, which focus the sun's rays like a giant magnifying glass, have been able to heat oil to three thousand degrees Celsius, which in turn can fuel steam turbines. More commonly, trough collectors have been used to heat oil to four hundred degrees Celsius, generating steam turbines. California's Mojave Desert currently produces two hundred megawatts of electricity using a series of thirty-megawatt collectors (Mathews 1989: Corson 1990; Weinberg and Williams 1991). The Luz Corporation is currently expanding its Mojave facility, bringing its planned output to six hundred megawatts (Corson 1990).

The limitations of solar thermal energy are that it requires a generally sunny climate, and trough systems require a substantial amount of space. Thus, solar thermal energy is not suitable everywhere. Still, in conjunction with other renewable energy technologies, solar thermal energy may make an effective contribution toward energy for the future.

Solar: Photovoltaic Cells

Photovoltaic (PV) cells directly convert sunlight into electricity, and their potential is almost unlimited. Worldwide, over fifteen thousand homes are supplied with PV-generated electricity (Corson 1990). A forty-square-meter network of 12 percent efficient PV cells will produce enough electricity for a single household (Weinberg and Williams 1991). And the necessary network size will become smaller as PV-cell efficiency increases. Current PV technologies allow for the manufacture of a 28.5 percent efficient point-contact crystalline silicon cell and a 35 percent efficient gallium arsenide-gallium-antimonide stacked junction cell—a double-layered cell that absorbs different aspects of the solar spectrum (Weinberg and Williams 1991). The largest single photovoltaic facility is a 6.5 megawatt plant in California's Carissa Plains run by ARCO solar (Corson 1990).

Photovoltaic cells produce electricity with zero emissions, are noise free, and require minimal maintenance. But they have two constraints. The present cost of PV-generated electricity—resulting from the manufacture of PV cells—is still about five times that of traditional sources, though costs have been dropping consistently since the 1970s (Weinberg and Williams 1991). Also, the manufacture of PV cells produces hazardous wastes that must be managed (Smith 1992).

Geothermal

Geothermal energy is created from the heat contained within the earth's interior. Geologic blowholes and volcanic activity illustrate the potential energy that can be harnessed. The electricity generated by geothermal sources worldwide was estimated to reach sixty-four hundred megawatts in 1990, equaling the output of six large nuclear power plants (WRI and IIED 1989; National Research Council 1987). The United States is currently generating about twenty-five hundred megawatts (Smith 1992).

There are currently around twenty nations exploring the geothermal option. Geologists estimate that geothermal power can be harnessed on approximately 10 percent of the earth's land (Smith 1992). Geothermal facilities may contribute a significant amount of renewable energy in the future. While highly sulfurous waste water and odors can result as a byproduct of the geothermal process, proper management of geothermal sources can minimize these problems.

Ocean Energy

Harnessing ocean energy is based on relatively new processes. The most promising technology is Ocean Thermal Energy Conversion (OTEC). OTEC exploits the temperature difference between warmer surface water and colder deep water to generate electricity. OTEC is still in its preliminary stages, but prototypes suggest that 100-megawatt plants will be feasible within several years (Corson 1990). Other ocean energy systems include the harnessing of wave and tidal power. Norway has made progress on prototype wave power plants, and France has a prototype tidal energy plant capable of producing 240 megawatts (Corson 1990).

Conservation

Though not a fuel as such, energy conservation will provide a net contribution to power needs and will improve environmental quality. Reducing energy consumption will result in reducing the number of plants needed, thereby decreasing emissions and reducing hazardous byproducts. Many communities do encourage various forms of conservation; however, much more can be done. Increasing insulation standards in all new commercial and residential building will result in a significant decrease in heating and cooling needs.

Similarly, mandating efficiency standards for energy-consuming products (from light bulbs to air conditioners) will both reduce energy needs and lengthen the usable life of products. In addition, cogeneration systems will allow steam produced for industry to heat surrounding areas and provide local electrical generation. The deficit in U.S. efficiency standards, compared to those of Japan and western Europe, suggests that much more can be accomplished (*Scientific American* 1991; Corson 1990; Smith 1992).

Integrated Energy Management

Few of the above options are problem free. However, with proper management, these renewable energy sources can replace the need for traditional fossil or nuclear fuel. No single energy source will solve our energy problems. But, by integrating the most efficient of these sources into a single energy network, while conserving to the maximum extent possible, these technologies will represent a significant improvement in environmental quality and in energy independence.

Conclusion

The failure to embrace clean, safe, and renewable energy sources in a substantive way can be tied directly to the Liberal tradition in the United States. The emphasis on individual self-interest over community interest makes the evolution of a comprehensive energy policy difficult. The constant drive for continual economic expansion that characterizes American liberalism places short-term economic gain above long-term environmental quality and the development of safe and renewable energy resources.

This chapter illustrated the tensions between liberalism and renewable clean energy. Traditional energy policies have been symbolic in two ways. First, in placing consumption over conservation, policy makers have encouraged the deeply rooted myth that energy resources are unlimited. Second, the environmental impact of energy production and use has consistently been ignored. These mechanisms accommodate the tension between liberalism and energy conservation. Table 7.3 illustrates a positive trend toward reducing per capita energy consumption since the mid-1980s, although overall energy consumption (Table 7.1) continues to grow. Future energy policies may further reduce per capita consumption, providing a foundation for energy and environmental security.

As in the other environmental policy areas, when policy makers consciously ignore the larger implications of wasteful consumption and environmental degradation, they are seeking to reinforce cultural myths at the expense of long-term environmental health. The following chapter brings together the questions that the entire study has raised, discussing the difficult choices Liberal society must address as it comes to terms with the environmental crisis.

8 Conclusion:
Options and Alternatives

Will mankind survive? Who knows? ... How many of us would be
willing to give up some minor convenience—say the use of
aerosols—in the hope that this might extend the life of man on earth
by a hundred years? Suppose we knew with a high degree of cer-
tainty that humankind could not survive a thousand years unless
we gave up our wasteful diet of meat, abandoned all pleasure dri-
ving, cut back on every use of energy that was not essential to that
maintenance of a bare minimum. Would we care enough for pos-
terity to pay the price of its survival?
—Robert Heilbroner 1980:179

Over the past two centuries, policy makers have been relatively successful in satisfying public expectations relative to communal problems.
This has been possible because the public has traditionally accepted the
distinction between public and private spheres. Citizens, as independent actors, have largely accepted responsibility for "private" crises.
That is, problems that affect people have been interpreted by most as
personal problems. Public problems have historically been defined as
structural in nature. Government has been expected only to maintain a
secure nation, free from external threats and economic instability. Since
1970, however, public demand has extended the discourse on common
good to include resource management and environmental protection.
The Santa Barbara oil spill in 1969, the toxic waste leaking from Love
Canal in 1978, the near core meltdown at Three Mile Island in 1978, the
chemical disaster in Bhopal, India, in 1984, the actual core meltdown at
Chernobyl in 1986, and the Valdez oil spill in 1989 have all helped trans-
form public expectations of communal responsibility.

The traditional accommodation to public demand has been symbolic policies that seek to satisfy public outcry. The environmental era

between 1969 and 1990 has been characterized by a strong policy agenda and weak policy implementation. The result has been a tenuous balance between environmental policy and public demand. As the dialectic between environmental degradation and expansionary fiscal policies continues, Liberal society must face some serious questions.

The tension between capitalism and environmental quality is inherent in the Liberal legacy contemporary society has inherited. Environmental degradation in the United States is largely a result of Liberal capitalism. Kann (1986) argues that

> to the extent the environment has been influenced in the United States it has been influenced by elites who exercise concentrated power on their own behalf. They pursue material wealth and systematically ignore the consequences of unrestrained economic growth on people's daily lives. (Kann 1986:253)

The framers of the Constitution were explicit in their desire to protect the rights of property owners to create wealth through the exploitation of natural resources. The result has been two centuries of environmental neglect.

As Liberal society comes to recognize the broader issues confronting it as communal issues, the discourse on communal good is likely to change. In order to improve environmental quality substantially, it is necessary to redefine traditional property rights to reflect the expanding arena of communal good. To the extent that Liberal economics has been predicated on a continually expanding production base, environmental resources have been overused and degraded. Relying on the "market" to monitor resource extraction and use has failed. The Liberal emphasis on individual good as the central criterion for environmental management has resulted in maximizing individual and corporate profit at the expense of communal good.

The Options Facing Liberal Society

As Liberal society comes to terms with the environmental crisis, it will face some difficult questions. The traditional attempt by policy makers to satisfy public demands, while simultaneously emphasizing Lockean property rights, has created an untenable policy structure for environmental improvement. To this point, the study has defined the parameters of the conflict between liberalism and environmental quality. The following section explores the options Liberal society faces through the conceptual framework of Hardin's (1968) "Tragedy of the Commons."

The Tragedy of the Commons

In "The Tragedy of the Commons" Hardin recreates the classic discussion on the conflict between individual rights and common good. Drawing from William Lloyd's 1833 pamphlet on population control, Hardin argues that individual self-interest is a poor tool for determining resource allocation. The "commons" refers to pasture lands that are open to all for the grazing of livestock. Hardin begins by explaining the impact of self-interested "herdsmen" on the commons.

As rational human beings, herdsmen will naturally seek to maximize their economic interest and will therefore graze as many head of livestock as they can. The benefit of grazing each additional animal will be enjoyed by the individual herdsman. The costs—for example, overgrazing—will be shared collectively. Thus, for each additional animal introduced, the individual herdsman will receive a benefit of +1. The cost, which Hardin values as −1, is divided among all herdsmen using the commons.

In this way each herdsman will maximize benefits while externalizing costs. The result, Hardin suggests, is that each herdsman, being equally rational, will seek to graze as many animals as possible. The outcome, not surprisingly, is the destruction of the commons and the starvation of each herdsman's livestock:

> Each man is locked into a system that compels him to increase his herd without limit—in a world that is limited. Ruin is the destination toward which all men rush, each pursuing his own best interest in a society that believes in the freedom of the commons. Freedom of the commons brings ruin to all. (Hardin 1968)

Hardin anticipates free-market environmentalism by suggesting that to avoid ruin, common resources must be allocated so that they can be controlled by individual private interests. The logic here is that each herdsman, given control of a plot of land, would balance his or her short-term self-interest of grazing additional animals with his or her long-term self-interest in sustaining the plot as productive pasture. He suggests that privatizing the commons might be done by selling off portions, by allocating portions based on merit, through a lottery, or simply through a first-come first-served basis. He finds each method of allocation equally objectionable but less objectionable than destruction of the commons itself.

Others (e.g., Heilbroner 1980) argue that the commons are already so degraded that some form of centralized management must be imposed. Clearly, herdsmen will put their own self-interest above the interests of society as a whole. They will, therefore, continue to deplete the pastures, even if the commons was divided among each user. This because the immediate short-term benefit to the individual herdsman outweighs the abstract long-term benefit to descendants and heirs.

There are, however, other options. A Rawlsian perspective might suggest that if the herdsmen were truly rational, maintaining the collective commons for long-term use would be understood as within the broad individual self-interest of each user. This might be accommodated in two ways. First, in recognizing the long-term interest in maintaining productive pastures, herdsmen might voluntarily limit the number of animals they graze. In this sense, they might embrace a model of self-regulation.

Were this to fail, perhaps due to the perception by individual users that other herdsmen may be overgrazing, it may be possible to create a mechanism whereby the state assumes regulatory responsibility to ensure the maintenance of productive pastures. In this way, Rawls' model may allow for a regulatory system that would protect the commons, thus maximizing the long-term self-interest of each herdsman.

The options illustrated in the commons discourse are precisely the options Liberal society now faces. Do we maintain a narrow self-interest model, with potentially disastrous results? If environmental degradation continues, will we be pushed toward a neo-Hobbesian model of severe environmental regulation—for example, eco-authoritarianism. Or will it be possible to move away from narrow self-interests in order to accommodate the environmental challenges? The sections below discuss these issues in greater detail.

Stay the Course

The simplest choice facing Liberal society, is, in the words of George Bush, to "stay the course." Economic elites have argued that Liberal capitalism is the best course for environmental improvement. Many point to the devastating environmental conditions in eastern Europe, particularly Rumania, and argue that centralized planning is no panacea. Economists such as Simon (1986) see technology as the answer to resource degradation. Rather than reduce consumption, Liberal society should look to advanced technology to solve environmental problems. And, they argue, only Liberal society is capable of spawning the necessary technological creativity to address the potential threat. Just as modern industrial technology is significantly cleaner than early technologies, future technology will be cleaner than today.

This analysis, however, confuses economic advancement with technological advancement. There is no definite correlation between maximizing profit (self-interest) and clean technologies. The reliance on fossil fuels, for example, betrays a commitment to a profitable though polluting technology, even though cleaner alternatives are available. Furthermore, the problem of communal good remains—and this may be the greater stumbling block. What mechanism will put communal good back into the Liberal stew?

Free-market environmentalists argue that narrow self-interest, itself, is the tool necessary for improving environmental quality. Like Hardin, they argue that property rights encourage responsible management. Property owners recognize the need to maintain the long-term value of property. Nature conservancies, for example, are private organizations that acquire land to set aside as nature reserves.

In addition, some free-market environmentalists argue that it is environmentally appropriate to encourage property rights because property owners can be held responsible for environmental degradation caused by the use of their property. Anderson and Leal (1991) describe a property rights approach to address mobile source air emissions. If highways were privatized and strict liability were enforced, highway owners would have an incentive to reduce emissions. They might achieve this by charging higher tolls for vehicles that lack appropriate pollution control equipment. The key is in making the polluter pay, whether the polluter be defined as the vehicle owner or as the highway owner. Preventing polluters from externalizing pollution costs creates an incentive to minimize emissions.

The question, ultimately, is whether liberalism can accommodate communal need. If free market approaches can be found to make property owners liable for pollution it is plausible that a free-market equilibrium can be sought to manage environmental claims. But, even if independent market-driven companies evolved to monitor pollution sources, some type of governmental intervention is necessary to enforce liability claims. This is not necessarily inconsistent with existing models of adjudication to settle competing property claims.[1]

The problem, however, is that in privatizing the commons—for example, highways, beaches, national parks, water sheds, aquifers, fresh air, and so forth—we would allow access according to economic criteria. In this way, resources that are critical for survival would be allocated on an ability-to-pay basis. In a sense, this would accommodate common good by eliminating the "common." Further, it eliminates any claim by those species of animals and plants that have no ability to participate in economic interactions.

The Environmental Leviathan

Heilbroner (1980) doubts that humankind has the empathetic power to voluntarily reduce consumption to improve environmental quality, regardless of the consequences for our children and grandchildren. As a result, he sees environmental degradation becoming so severe that citizens will need to submit to a neo-Hobbesian state, where an environmental Leviathan will be necessary to resolve the environmental crisis.

Depending on the environmental challenge, Democratic politics may indeed be replaced by authoritarian structures. A catastrophe on the level of Bhopal or Chernobyl would certainly bring the imposition of emergency powers to meet the threat. But, precluding a tragic environmental accident, is an environmental Leviathan necessary or desirable? Heilbroner's pronouncement, that when left to its own devices human nature is incapable of avoiding doom, may or may not be correct. But, even if true, facing certain doom is not necessarily sufficient reason to abandon democratic principles. In a sense, to paraphrase Israeli poet Amos Oz, a free people has the power to avoid calamity—or head right into it. If human nature is so shortsighted as to place immediate gratification over human survival, perhaps there is little reason to savor posterity. Human survival is based on collective responsibility, not on philosopher kings or Fascists.

The potential for an environmental Leviathan to evolve rests on the extent to which environmental problems are neglected, and thus are allowed to grow. Ophuls (1977) and Milbrath (1989) argue that Liberal society can avoid the need for authoritarianism by creating a sustainable society.

The Sustainable Society

Ophuls has argued that avoiding the environmental Leviathan will require the creation of the "steady state," based on a sustainable economy. Milbrath argues similarly, pointing out that "avoiding change will make us victims of change" (1989:341). The earth has a remarkably large capacity to absorb waste, but not an unlimited capacity. Herman Daly (1991) describes the environmental problem with expansionary economics this way:

> Consider a boat. Suppose we want to maximize the load that the boat carries. If we place all the weight in one corner of the boat it

will quickly sink or capsize. Therefore, we spread the weight out evenly. To do this we may create a pricing system. The heavier the load in one part of the boat the higher the price of adding another pound in that place. We allocate the weight so as to equalize the cost per additional capacity used in all parts of the boat. . . . This pricing rule is an allocative mechanism only, a useful but dumb computer algorithm that sees no reason not to keep adding weight and allocating it optimally until the optimally loaded boat sinks, optimally of course, to the bottom of the sea. What is lacking is an absolute limit on scale. . . . Pricing is only a tool for finding optimal allocation. . . . The market by itself has no criterion by which to limit its scale relative to its environment. (Daly 1991:190)

If expansionary capitalism is inconsistent with environmental quality, environmental improvement may only be possible through an economic system that brings consumption and waste into equilibrium with the resource capacity of the ecosystem. The move to a sustainable society requires a shift in existing belief systems. Limiting consumption and economic expansion is antithetical to dominant ideals and values. Consequently, moving toward the sustainable society requires a fundamental shift in the way Americans think. Ophuls and Milbrath argue that Liberal society has little choice; as difficult as it may be, a paradigm shift is necessary if we are to be masters of our own fate.

The sustainable society, however, may be the least likely alternative that Liberal society would take. As rational as it may be, it is inconsistent with traditional Liberal culture. It is more plausible that liberalism will slowly evolve to accommodate the sharpest edges of environmental degradation, though perhaps too slowly. This, of course, is the fear of Ophuls and Milbrath. Still, paradigm shifts are possible, and environmental degradation may be enough to reorder the priorities of Liberal society.

Rawls and the Move toward Environmental Liberalism

Rawls (1971) argues that justice must be a central priority in liberalism. Rawls accepts self-interest as the primary social influence, while rejecting the utilitarian character that has come to dominate Western liberalism. To incorporate a notion of justice, Rawls broadens the self-interest model to accommodate a communitarian ethic:

each person is to have an equal right to the most extensive basic liberty compatible with a similar liberty for others; [and] social and economic inequalities are to be arranged so that they are both (a) reasonably expected to be to everyone's advantage, and (b) attached to positions and offices open to all. (Rawls 1971:60)

Further, Rawls defines just policies as those that benefit the least advantaged within the society, in addition to anyone else. Rawls' concept of fairness and of *pareto optimality* are useful for expanding the traditionally narrow self-interest model. Specifically, policies are fair when they make some people better off without at the same time making other people worse off. This is within the self-interest model—albeit a broader self-interest model—because "fair" policies protect the interests of each person. Self-interest itself includes maximizing social goods and minimizing social bads. Environmental protection, in this sense, maximizes social goods— clean air, clean water, healthy beaches and so forth—and minimizes social bads—environmental degradation.

But the Rawlsian approach is not problem free. Wenz (1988) points out that, like the model of free-market environmentalism discussed above, Rawls' theory is unable to account for justice to nonhuman constituents. Even within Rawls concept of justice, there is little to protect the self-interest of plants, wildlife, and other natural resources when it comes into conflict with the self-interest of human beings. Like other forms of liberalism, Rawls is inherently anthropocentric.

Paehlke (1989) and Orr (1992) may make up for Rawls' environmental shortcomings. Paehlke suggests that environmentalism may introduce a new paradigm, neither Liberal nor Marxist, that takes off where Rawls ends. Orr argues that an ecocentric analysis of our world is essential to maintain long-term survival.

In *Environmentalism and the Future of Progressive Politics*, Paehlke suggests that environmentalism may compete with liberalism in defining future options. In order to compete with liberalism, environmentalism, as an ideology—"a set of political ideals, a worldview both value laden and comprehensive"—must develop clear positions on the entire range of social and political issues (Paehlke 1989:3–5). In this way, an ecocentric world view may offer an alternative to Liberal assumptions on a range of issues, including unemployment, feminism, social programs, national defense, and the economy.

The environmental ideology, as Paehlke defines it, replaces the Liberal self-interest model with a common interest model centered around maximizing environmental quality:

The first principle of environmentalism is that the earth-as-a-whole, for all time, must be seen as a "commons." Environmentalism grants both other species and future human generations consideration in economic and resource decisions. (Paehlke 1989:8)

The success of environmentalism, Paehlke argues, is based on its ability to resurrect progressive politics in the United States. Because environmentalism is compatible with progressive politics in a variety of ways—enhancing governmental regulation to protect a public good, balancing economic growth with humanistic concerns, encouraging increased investment in education, social welfare, the arts, and health, and in challenging the hegemony of the market economy—green politics may absorb the energy and constituency of the progressive camps (Paehlke 1989:276–77).

Yet, Paehlke's notion of an "environmentally informed progressivism" distinguishes itself from traditional progressivism, seeking environmental protection even at the risk of alienating traditionally progressive constituencies—such as labor unions. It may promote technological transformations resulting in automation and the demise of dirty industries; it may promote the elimination of government deficits; it promotes small and medium-scale entrepreneurship; and, it may encourage a reduced work week in order to achieve full employment (Paehlke 1989:277). Thus, Paehlke suggests that many "neo-conservatives" (Liberals) may find a place within an emerging environmental paradigm. The ideology of environmentalism may simply be the result of self-interested people recognizing the long-term benefit of survival.

But, while the ranks of environmentalists have been growing, widespread acceptance of environmental ideals may require a systematic environmental education. Orr suggests that this is possible through a systematic reordering of priorities to create ecological literacy. This will only come about through educating people on what they "need to know to live responsibly and well in a finite world" (Orr 1992:133):

> The historic upheavals in the Soviet Union and Eastern Europe in 1989–1990 are ample evidence that communism, or at least a particular version of it, has failed. We have to admit that Western capitalism has failed as well. Our failures are still concealed by bad book-keeping (both fiscal and ecological), dishonest rhetoric, and wishful thinking. . . . Communism has all but collapsed because it could not produce enough; capitalism is failing because it produces too much and shares too little. . . . Neither system is sustainable in either human or ecological terms. We now face the task of rebuilding something different, a postmodern world that pro-

tects individual rights while protecting the larger interests of the planet and our children who live on it. (Orr 1992:ix)

Orr argues that as people come to realize the failure of capitalism—through the process of environmental consciousness raising—the ideals of the "postmodern world" will gain salience. Thus, for Orr, like Paehlke, ecocentric education becomes a dynamic for social evolution.

Civic Virtue and the Future of Liberalism

It is likely that Liberal society will adapt to meet the threat of catastrophic environmental degradation. The question is whether or not Liberal society will adapt in time. Milbrath's admonition to be masters of change rather than victims of change is most relevant here. This study has argued that liberalism is fundamentally incompatible with environmental improvement. It is therefore unlikely that Liberal society will undergo the wholesale paradigm shift that Milbrath anticipates.

More likely, as Liberal society confronts the severity of environmental degradation, it will rediscover an evolving notion of communal good. In this sense, American society may move toward a culture where individual self-interest is tempered with communal responsibility. This might be Rawlsian liberalism, or in Orr's paradigm, postmodernism. Whatever we might call it, it suggests a redefinition of traditional Liberal values.

There is a hint of such a move within the Clinton rhetoric, but it is subtle and ambiguous. While Americans are hesitant to change, there is a recognition that the world around us has already changed. That is, with the hazards created by industrial society, traditional property rights may pose tragic new threats to communal good (e.g., the Bhopal disaster).

Paehlke and Orr argue that environmentalism may be the dynamic that pushes liberalism to integrate its emphasis on individual self-interest with a more meaningful notion of common interest. Thus, liberalism may come to adopt environmental quality as an ethic. In such a way, the communal good of environmental sustenance will come to be an element of Liberal self-interest. This is distinct from "staying the course" in that rather than waiting for technology to rescue Liberal society from environmental doom, it allows the re-emergence of civic virtue as an important criterion in public policy decisions. The inclusion of civic virtue creates a post-Liberal society—one that includes in its assumptions a recognition that communal good is as necessary as individual good and communal rights as necessary as individual rights.

Overcoming Symbolic Action

Still, any social or cultural transition will continue to be inhibited by symbolic action. Citizens are, as Chapter 2 discusses at length, especially vulnerable to simplistic condensations of reality and reassuring messages from policy elites. Social change, as a consequence, can only come with a new awareness by the public that "business as usual" poses a serious threat to the social and economic well-being of the nation.

To the extent that personal experience will overshadow symbolic action in the development of political cognitions, environmental degradation may be the tension that erodes the symbolic accommodation. As millions of people share the experience of increasingly toxic air and water pollution, personal references may no longer be consistent with the symbolic image of environmental improvement suggested by policy elites. As such, symbolic policies may no longer be sufficient to quell public arousal.

The options Liberal society chooses in confronting the environmental crisis are, in large measure, related to the extent the power of symbolic action can be eroded. If continuing environmental degradation sparks enough discontent, Liberal society may be more likely to adopt substantive policies to confront the environmental challenge. There are existing policy models that would clearly result in substantial environmental improvement. The question remains, however, as to the costs Liberal society is prepared to accept for environmental improvement.

Clinton and the Liberal Legacy:
Environmental Policy in the 1990s

The 1992 election brought a new approach to American politics. After twelve years of Reagan and Bush, the Clinton-Gore administration has ushered in a new attitude about federal policy making. Clinton was elected on a platform of "people first," a significant departure from the politics of neglect of the 1980s. If the Reagan and Bush administrations were based on limiting federal involvement in solving problems, the Clinton administration has assembled an impressive brain trust to help identify proactive policies that confront problems directly.

Nonetheless, both Clinton and Gore have accepted the Liberal assumptions of the Reagan revolution. Specifically, Clinton has argued, even more persuasively than Reagan or Bush, that market incentives can be harnessed to solve social problems (e.g., Clinton and Gore 1992).

In this sense, Clinton is as much a Liberal as his predecessors. He too sees the main role of government as protecting individual self-interest. As a consequence, the Clinton-Gore administration will not ease the tension between liberalism and environmental quality. While they certainly will improve the federal government's role in protecting the environment, the fundamental conflicts will stay in place.

Clinton has been successful in touching on the concerns of the public. Similarly, he is aware of the policies necessary to achieve a substantive improvement in environmental quality. During the 1992 campaign Clinton outlined an environmental policy approach based on mass transit, conservation, renewable energy, resource reduction and recovery, and ultimately, better control of hazardous materials. But, rather than impose such policies, Clinton favors creating market incentives that will encourage these programs. This, unfortunately, is his environmental downfall. This study has argued that there is an insurmountable conflict between economics as usual and environmental protection. Clinton is proposing that we use economics as usual in a manner that best suits environmental sustenance.

The result, I believe, will be disappointing. Implementing programs such as mass transit, renewable energy research and development, and waste reduction will require a significant transition in our economic system. Viable public transportation systems are enormously expensive and will require a significant revenue source—possibly a federal gas tax or highway user fees. Renewable energy technologies are not only costly, they challenge the economic hegemony of traditional energy companies; strong opposition, therefore, can be anticipated. Significantly reducing waste will require much more than a federal recycling program, it will require a shift away from consumption—and consequently from consumer capitalism.

Trends in the Clinton Administration

The Clinton administration has brought a fresh perspective to environmental protection. Throughout the 1992 campaign, Clinton identified the need to address environmental concerns aggressively. The selection of Al Gore as vice-president may have been, at least in part, a symbolic gesture, but it does suggest that he is genuinely concerned about environmental quality. Gore's book *Earth in the Balance*[2] (1992) calls for civilization to "restore the balance" between human needs and environmental needs.

The environmental plan outlined during the 1992 Clinton campaign contains an ambitious environmental agenda, including reducing solid and hazardous waste through conservation and expanded recycling markets; preserving wetland and wilderness areas; creating economic incentives for maintaining environmental quality; exerting American leadership for improving global environmental quality; and increasing energy efficiency and conservation. Clinton's plan favors increasing the corporate average fuel economy standards (CAFE standards) from the current 27.5 mpg to 40 mpg, and he recognizes the need to encourage the further development of mass transit systems. Similarly, he favors higher efficiency in building materials and appliances (Clinton and Gore 1992). In his first State of the Union Address Clinton unveiled a plan to tax energy use. The BTU tax would have made a significant contribution to conservation, but, ultimately, was blocked by Congress. The only surviving remnant of his energy tax is a 4.3-cent-per-gallon addition to the gasoline tax, a meager if incremental increase.

Clinton's EPA administrator Carol Browner has a positive record as head of Florida's Department of Environmental Regulation (Kenworthy 1992). And, Clinton has stated his intention of elevating EPA to a cabinet-level department (Abramson 1993). Clinton's secretary of interior, Bruce Babbitt, was president of the League of Conservation Voters and has a strong environmental record as Governor of Arizona (Kenworthy 1993). Babbit may represent Clinton's most successful environmental advocate. He has already taken on strong western senators, announcing plans to double the fee for grazing animals on public land.

But, in the first year of his presidency, Clinton has delayed actively pursuing his environmental strategies. His environmental plan has yet to be explained fully, and there are no substantive environmental policy proposals on the horizon. While the economic problems Clinton has inherited have clearly taken priority, his ability to balance the consumption/conservation dilemma will determine his environmental success.

Clinton remains committed to environmental improvement—at least rhetorically—but there are troubling trends. Upon taking office Clinton declared that the deficit was more severe than anticipated, and consequently his policy proposals would have to wait (Phillips 1993). The appointment of O'Leary as DOE secretary has environmentalists concerned. The drive to "reinvent government," and the consequential replacement of the Council on Environmental Quality (CEQ) with the White House Office of Environmental Policy—a smaller, lower funded agency—has highlighted the apparent contradiction between expanding regulatory responsibility while simultaneously reducing regulatory agency staff. And, the Clinton administration has been unusually slow in making regulatory appointments to EPA, particularly regional administrators.

Clinton's Pacific Northwest forest agreement and the North American Free Trade Agreement (NAFTA) elicited more substantive criticism from the environmental community. The forest agreement seeks to break the impasse between environmentalists and the timber industry. The plan would allow loggers into limited areas in the last ancient forests, though forest reserves around watersheds and reduced logging on federal lands would offset some of the damage. Further, the plan allows salvage logging within the reserves and reduces riparian protection around surface waters and wetlands.

NAFTA, though endorsed by some environmental organizations, may create a mechanism to challenge U.S. environmental laws as restraints to trade. Laws regulating air and water, pesticide controls, wildlife protection, recycling programs, and energy conservation may have to be scaled back if they are found to interfere with the intent of the trade agreement (Benson 1993).

While Clinton may have a sincere interest in improving environmental quality, his policy priorities, like those of his predecessors, focus on economic growth. The NAFTA debate illustrates the tensions between economic issues, such as free trade, and environmental regulation. However, Clinton cannot ignore environmental issues. Environmental quality remains a salient issue within the constituency that elected him. Thus, while economic issues have taken priority during the recessionary period of his early presidency, he may come to address environmental issues more aggressively later in his term.

The transition to the environmental policy framework outlined by Clinton and Gore in *Putting People First* (1992) will require bold leadership. Considering current economic constraints and the market philosophy of the Clinton administration, it is unlikely that environmental policy in the 1990s will be characterized by a Paehlke/Orr model of ecocentrism. Rather, an incremental model of environmental policy reminiscent of the Nixon, Ford, and Carter years is more likely to evolve. Thus, while there may be significant improvement in environmental policy making relative to the last twelve years, the underlying problems will persist.

Public Policies for Environmental Quality: A Practical Guide

There is little question that environmental conditions will require a substantial revision in the way Americans live, as it already has in many places. While the future may offer numerous unknowns, specific technologies and policies already exist which will help reduce environmental damage in years to come. The following is an overview of these policies.

Mass Transit

By far the most far-reaching change in American society will be the way people commute from place to place. Automobiles are one of the main sources of air and water pollution. Vehicle traffic alone accounts for more than 36 percent of airborne pollutants (EPA 1989a). Hydrocarbons are emitted into the air, and rubber and oil deposits from roadways are ultimately washed into surface waters with rain runoff (Rosenbaum 1991).

Mass transportation systems will reduce pollution, relieve congestion, lower noise levels, and ultimately improve commute times between destinations. Specific proposals to get people out of their automobiles and into public transit include additional fuel taxes, higher tolls, and closing some urban areas (such as downtown Los Angeles) to cars during peak hours. The resulting funds can then be used to subsidize public transit, improving systems and reducing fares (Associated Press 1989; Wald 1989).

Energy Conservation and Alternatives

Energy conservation is also a basic element in preserving environmental quality. While most people think of electricity as a clean energy source, coal, diesel fuel, and nuclear utilities are major contributors to environmental degradation. Reducing energy consumption will result in reducing the number of plants needed, decreased emissions, and a reduction in radioactive wastes (*Scientific American* 1991; Corson 1990).

Many communities are encouraging various forms of conservation; however, much more can be done. Increasing insulation standards in all new commercial and residential building will result in a significant decrease in heating and cooling needs. Similarly, mandating efficiency standards for energy consuming products will both reduce energy needs and lengthen the usable life of products. Alternative energy sources, such as methane and alcohol mixtures, are both renewable and cleaner than petroleum-based fuels. A shift from fossil fuel dependency to renewable sources will not only reduce U.S. reliance on foreign supplies, but will also provide a cleaner environment (WRI and IIED 1987, 1989).

Emission Controls

The hallmarks of existing environmental policy models are specific emissions quality standards. These standards need to be strengthened and enforced rigorously. Existing standards are relatively weak, compliance deadlines have been continually postponed, and the EPA infrastructure to implement these programs has been seriously inadequate. A commitment to environmental quality necessitates a commitment to implementing effective regulatory policy. Also, regulatory policy can be expanded beyond existing coercive models. Rational strategies to maximize compliance can be developed using a variety of regulatory devices (Cohen and Kamieniecki 1991). In addition to traditional command and control policies, economic incentives to reduce pollution output may be effective. Such incentives include charging polluters an emissions tax, making it cheaper to retrofit equipment and possibly reduce production than to pay extra taxes (Rosenbaum 1991; Portney 1990).

Source Reduction (Precycling)

A major element of improving environmental quality is reducing the extraction of limited resources. More efficient energy standards will result in fewer resources used. Energy standards resulting in an increased longevity of consumer goods will reduce the constant need to replace products. Mandating a reduction in packaging of consumer goods, which currently accounts for 50 percent of municipal landfills, will cut solid waste significantly (Pollock 1987).

Resource Recovery (Recycling)

Recycling has been a basic element of life for most generations. Only recently has it been cheaper to throw away used resources than to clean and reuse them. To foster recycling, manufacturers must be required to incorporate post- consumer waste into new products. This might take the form of taxing virgin materials such as petroleum and timber pulp products. A national recycling program would result in saving resources, reducing energy used for processing and manufacturing and reducing solid waste (Earth Works Group 1990).

Resource Management

Existing resource management is split between private and governmental agencies. Property owners have traditionally been free to use their resources as they saw fit. Similarly, public resources administered by the departments of Interior, Energy, Agriculture, Defense, and Commerce have been managed according to the needs of economic development. The lack of a comprehensive resource management plan has left federal agencies vulnerable to economic interests. The Department of Interior has typically seen itself as an agency representing ranching and mineral interests, while the Department of Energy has identified its role as encouraging energy development in partnership with private and public energy companies. The Department of Agriculture has been concerned with corporate farming. The Defense Department has pursued weapons programs and combat training without regard for environmental consequences. Only the Commerce Department, through the U.S. Coast Guard, has seen a role for itself in protecting environmental quality. Long-term resource management can only come through a comprehensive plan which establishes specific priorities and thereby arbitrates between competing needs with long-term environmental quality in mind.

Integrated Waste Management

Integrated waste management is, in many ways, a combination of all the above programs. Integrated waste management is a system of precycling, recycling, composting, and processing the remaining waste into a compact, safely disposable, inert material. First and foremost, waste must be reduced to a manageable level. The longstanding human habit of burying waste in landfills and then moving when resources are used up is no longer tenable. Reducing waste through conservation (precycling) is the first step to responsible waste management. Then recycling allows the reusable resources to be removed, sorted, and processed. Organic material can then be removed and composted, allowing organic bacteria to digest composted waste and create a mineral-rich mulch which can be used as fertilizer. Composting essentially speeds up the biodegrading process and allows biodegraded material to be reused. Processing the remaining waste into compact, inert material is perhaps the most difficult prospect. New technologies suggest that incineration may be the solution, although most people are suspicious considering the dubious history of burning trash. New models of incineration, however, suggest that proper burning techniques reduce emissions and toxicity of the remaining ash. The key is the removal of nonburnable resources such as metal, glass, and plastics, and burning the waste at high temperatures (near twenty-four hundred degrees Fahrenheit) (WRI and IIED 1987; Corson 1990).

Sorting out recyclables (including metals, glass, and plastics) and compostable organics leaves a burnable material which can be used to fuel power plants, reducing reliance on coal and oil even further. In California's central valley, for example, a fifteen megawatt utility generates electricity by burning 7 million tons of used vehicle tires a year (Corson 1990). The remaining ash is then landfilled in specially lined facilities or suspended in an inert substance and then landfilled. While burning waste will result in some emissions, the exhaust is less damaging than burning coal and provides the same electrical output. The result is a savings in net emissions and a significant reduction in landfilled waste (Corson 1990; O'Leary 1988).

Where We Go from Here

This study has explored the specific tensions between liberalism and environmental quality and the symbolic accommodations made to that tension in environmental policy making. Further, the study has identified specific programs that would offer substantive alternatives to the existing policy models. At this point it is appropriate to discuss where research should go from here.

First and foremost, it would be helpful to explore state and local policy models, collecting comparative data to identify the evolution of any trends. For example, are citizens at the local level incorporating a notion of communal good into neighborhood programs? Recycling programs offer a good research tool in this regard. Furthermore, it would be beneficial to explore the correlation between resource degradation and environmentalism on the local level. Are those cities that are more polluted, such as Los Angeles, also more environmentally concerned? Similarly, in those communities which have experienced environmental catastrophes, such as Niagara County, New York (Love Canal, Bloody Run), and Woburn, Massachusetts, are citizens becoming active in environmental politics?

Another level of research that would be productive is the comparative study of cross-national environmental policies. Which nations are most effective in maintaining or improving environmental quality, and what are their policy models? Moreover, are there any cultural or political factors which contribute to environmental policy success or failure? This study, of course, argued that political economy is a major factor in environmental degradation. Now that the normative parameters of the discussion are laid out, it would be appropriate to test the hypothesis systemically on a cross-national level.

And, finally, is there any correlation between economics and environmental quality? This can be studied on a variety of levels. First, it is possible to examine communities in economically productive and depressed areas across the nation, using environmental quality, opinion on environmental issues, and ultimately local environmental policies as indicators. Second, similar research would be appropriate on the national level, using time series designs. Historically, environmental advocacy has been a luxury. Is this still the case? Or has continued environmental degradation made the environment an issue that crosses economic boundaries?

The central thesis of the study—that the emphasis on individual self-interest in Liberal society precludes resolving communal problems—is relevant to several policy areas in addition to the environment. Medical policy is experiencing similar tensions, as is labor policy, welfare policy, and education policy. The traditional reliance on health care as an economic commodity precludes the delivery of health services to the population as a whole.

Similarly, unemployment and underemployment are still identified as individual problems, making a policy resolution impossible. As a consequence of the Liberal assumption that all people are free to sell their labor at market value, as all employers are free to purchase labor at market value, unemployment appears to be an individual circumstance. As long as work is seen as a commodity, rather than a right, unemployment will persist.

Social welfare programs are at odds with the Liberal tradition. Since individual initiative is the core of Liberal society, poverty is seen as the result of individual laziness, not social dysfunction. As a consequence, Liberal societies develop social welfare programs grudgingly and with an element of punitiveness. That is, since welfare recipients are somehow responsible for their circumstances, the role of government is only to keep them alive. This attitude precludes effective social programs that might actually help people attain the services necessary to be integrated into the economic fabric in a meaningful way. Such programs include relevant job training, child care, health care, jobs programs—for example, paid apprenticeships, and career counseling.

Public education has long been recognized as critical for the long-term social and economic success of society. At the same time, liberalism has little language for defining a meaningful role for public education. Traditionally, liberalism placed the responsibility of educating and training children at home. American liberalism is therefore heir to two competing philosophies. As a consequence, the role of public education has been limited. Parents are responsible for providing a home environment consistent with their family's educational goals. Schools provide a limited common educational experience. The low funding of public schools reflects this assumption. Those families that are fortunate enough to have disposable income are in a much better position to provide supplemental educational opportunities for their children and to assist their children's schools. Liberalism's inability to define a common interest in raising the quality of public education precludes the investment necessary to improve schools—through such mechanisms as reducing class size, improving salaries to attract the highest caliber teachers, and improving access to appropriate materials and resources.

A Final Word

There is a curious irony between the apparent success of capitalism worldwide and the increasing global effort to improve environmental quality. These are, in many ways, two divergent trends. Environmental improvement can only come from a policy structure that acknowledges the importance of communal interest. As such, the renewed emphasis on Capitalist development worldwide may slow efforts at global environmentalism.

Still, there is widespread concern for degrading environmental conditions and for environmentally related threats to public health. The severity of environmental problems worldwide is only now beginning to be understood, and the extent of environmental calamity in countries like Rumania provides a strong reminder of our potential future. Consequently, as Milbrath (1989) points out, the role of researchers in educating the public has never been more important.

With this in mind, the environmental arena provides an excellent model of how formal scholarship, such as political science, can rejoin the political discourse. It is not enough to merely measure and report the state of the world; it is necessary to understand where we are going and identify the dynamics to avoid calamity. Or, as Marx wrote more bluntly, it is not enough to understand the world—the point is to change it.

Appendix 1

Federal Environmental Policy Summary, 1969–1992

Legislation	Summary
National Environmental Policy Act (NEPA), 1969; PL 91-190	Created Council on Environmental Quality; requires federal Environmental Impact Statements.
Resource Recovery Act, 1970; PL 91-512	Established grants for innovative solid waste management systems and provided technical aid to state and local agencies in creating waste disposal and recycling systems.
Clean Air Act, 1970; PL 91-604	Required EPA to establish national ambient air quality standards and emission limits; required states to create implementation plans by specific dates.
Clean Water Act, 1972; PL 92-500	Set national water quality standards; established pollution-discharge permit system; increased federal grants to states to build waste water treatment facilities.
Federal Environmental Pesticides Control Act, 1972; PL 92-516	Required registration of all pesticides commercially available in the United States; allowed EPA to suspend registration under specific circumstances.
Marine Protection Act, 1972; PL 92-532	Regulated dumping of waste into the oceans and coastal waters.
Coastal Zone Management Act, 1972; PL 92-583	Created federal grants to help states develop coastal zone management plans under federal guidelines.

(continued)

Legislation	*Summary*
Endangered Species Act, 1973; PL 93-205	Broadened federal authority to protect all "threatened" and "endangered" species; authorized grants to assist states; required coordination among all federal agencies.
Safe Drinking Water Act, 1974; PL 93-523	Required EPA to set standards of public drinking water supplies and to regulate state programs for protecting groundwater.
Toxic Substances Control Act (TSCA), 1976; PL 94-469	Authorized EPA to pre-market test all chemical substances; allowed EPA to regulate or ban any chemical presenting an "unreasonable risk of injury to health or environment"; prohibited most uses of PCBs.
Federal Land Policy Management Act, 1976; PL 94-579	Gave BLM authority to manage public lands for long-term benefits; ended policy of conveying public lands into private ownership.
Resource Conservation and Recovery Act (RCRA), 1976; PL 94-580	Required EPA to set regulations for hazardous waste treatment, storage, transportation, and disposal; provided assistance for state hazardous waste programs; established standards for solid waste disposal; required Commerce Department to encourage markets for recycled materials and the development of waste recovery technologies.
National Forest Management Act, 1976; PL 94-588	Gave statutory permanence to national forest lands and set new standards for their management; restricted timber harvesting to protect soil and watersheds; limited clearcutting.
Surface Mining Control and Reclamation Act (SMCRA), 1977; PL 95-87	Set environmental controls over strip mining; limited mining on farmland, alluvial valleys, and slopes; required restoration of land to original contours.
Clean Air Act Amendments, 1977; PL 95-95	Amended 1970 Clean Air Act by postponing deadlines for compliance with auto emissions and air quality stan-

(*continued*)

Legislation	*Summary*
	dards; set new standards for "prevention of significant deterioration" of clean air areas.
Clean Water Act Amendments, 1977; PL 95-217	Amended 1972 Clean Water Act by extending deadlines for industry and cities to meet waste water treatment standards; set national standards for industrial pretreatment of waste water; increased funding for sewage treatment construction grants, and gave states flexibility in determining priorities.
Public Utility Regulatory Policies Act, 1978; PL 95-617	Authorized Energy Department and Federal Energy Regulatory Commission to regulate electrical and natural gas utilities and crude oil transportation systems in order to promote energy conservation and efficiency; allowed small cogeneration and renewable energy projects to sell power to utilities.
Alaska National Interest Lands Conservation Act, 1980; PL 96-487	Protected 102 million acres of Alaskan land as national wilderness, wildlife refuges, and parks.
Comprehensive Environmental Response, Compensation, and Liability Act, 1980; PL 96-510	Authorized $1.6 billion "Superfund" to clean up chemical dump sites and hazardous waste emergencies.
Nuclear Waste Policy Act, 1982; PL 97-425; Nuclear Waste Policy Act Amendments, 1987; PL 100-203	Created a national plan for the permanent disposal of highly radioactive nuclear waste; authorized Energy Department to build and operate geologic repositories for spent fuel from commercial nuclear power plants.
Resource Conservation and Recovery Act Amendments, 1984; PL 98-616	Revised and strengthened EPA procedures for regulating hazardous waste facilities; authorized grants to states for management of solid waste and hazardous wastes; prohibited land disposal of certain hazardous liquid wastes; required states to consider re-

(*continued*)

Legislation	Summary
	cycling in comprehensive solid waste plans.
Food Security Act (Farm Bill), 1985; PL 99-198	Limited federal program benefits for producers of commodities on highly erodible land or converted wetlands; authorized Agriculture Department to provide technical assistance for sub-surface water quality preservation; revised and extended Soil and Water Conservation Act (1977) programs through 2008.
Safe Drinking Water Act, 1986; PL 99-339	Reauthorized the Safe Drinking Water Act of 1974 and revised EPA safe drinking water programs, including grants to states for drinking water standards enforcement and ground-water protection programs; accelerated EPA schedule for establishing standards for maximum contaminant levels for eighty-three toxic pollutants.
Superfund Amendments and Reauthorization Act, 1986; PL 99-499	Increased Superfund authorization from $1.6 billion to $8.5 billion through 1991 to clean up the nation's most dangerous abandoned waste sites; set strict standards and time-tables for cleaning up sites; required that industry provide local communities with information on chemicals used and emitted.
Clean Water Act Amendments, 1987; PL 100-4	Amended the Clean Water Acts of 1972 and 1977 and revised EPA water pollution control programs, including authorizing further grants to states for construction of waste water treatment facilities and implementation of mandated nonpoint-source pollution (e.g., runoff) management plans; expanded EPA enforcement authority; created a national estuary protection program.
Global Climate Protection Act, 1987; PL 100-204	Authorized the State Department to study the problems of global climate change; created an intergovernmental

(*continued*)

Legislation	Summary
	task force to develop a U.S. strategy for dealing with the threat posed by global warming.
Ocean Dumping Act, 1988; PL 100-688	Amended the Marine Protection Act (1972) to end all ocean disposal of sewage sludge and industrial waste by December 31, 1991; revised EPA ocean dumping regulations and established dumping fees, permit requirements, and civil penalties for violations.
Oil Pollution Prevention, Response, Liability, and Compensation Act, 1990; PL 101-380	Increased liability limits for oil spill cleanup costs; required double hulls for oil tankers and barges by 2015; required increased contingency planning and preparation for spills.
Pollution Prevention Act, 1990; PL 101-508	Established Office of Pollution Prevention in EPA to coordinate efforts at source reduction; mandated source reduction and recycling report to accompany annual toxics release under SARA.
Clean Air Act, 1990; PL 101-549	Revises expired Clean Air Act of 1970, setting new requirements and deadlines for compliance with air quality standards; mandates more stringent emission standards, new automobile pollution controls, and renewable fuel standards for new car fleets; reauthorizes industrial pollution controls, which must meet "best available technology" criteria; required reduction in sulfur dioxide and nitrogen oxides by power plants to reduce acid precipitation; required regulation of toxic and hazardous emissions, and regulated 189 chemicals; prohibited use of CFCs by 2000; phased out other ozone-depleting chemicals.
Energy Policy Act, 1992; PL 102-240	Aimed at reducing U.S. dependency on imported oil; restructured utilities to promote competition; promotes renewable energy for cars; eased licensing requirements for nuclear power

(*continued*)

Federal Environmental Policy Summary, 1969–1992 (*continued*)

Legislation	Summary
	plants; authorizes energy research and development.
Omnibus Water Act, 1992; PL 102-575	Authorized completion of major Western water projects; requires California's Central Valley Project (CVP) to allow transfer of water to urban areas; encourages conservation through a tiered pricing system; mandated additional wildlife and environmental protection and restoration.

Sources: Norman Vig and Michael Kraft, *Environmental Policy in the 1990s*, 1994, 2nd ed. (Washington, DC: Congressional Quarterly Press), appendix 1; Walter A. Rosenbaum, *Environmental Politics and Policy*, 1991, 2nd ed. (Washington, D.C.: Congressional Quarterly Press).

Appendix 2

Toxic Pollution Released by Manufacturing Industries, 1988 (by State)

State	Total Release (pounds)	Rank
Alabama	84,062,842	22
Alaska	26,476,465	38
American Samoa	29,500	53
Arizona	74,657,306	24
Arkansas	72,272,458	25
California	201,568,789	9
Colorado	21,132,981	42
Connecticut	53,449,946	30
Delaware	10,692,005	46
District of Columbia	1,000	54
Florida	249,655,746	6
Georgia	131,410,860	18
Hawaii	2,964,331	49
Idaho	15,105,613	44
Illinois	251,302,153	5
Indiana	276,346,921	4
Iowa	58,668,674	28
Kansas	174,468,243	13
Kentucky	131,319,642	19
Louisiana	741,206,814	1
Maine	21,965,123	41
Maryland	33,340,174	36
Massachusetts	70,821,565	26
Michigan	231,681,301	8
Minnesota	65,506,519	27
Mississippi	120,820,916	20
Missouri	184,627,555	12
Montana	35,467,330	34
Nebraska	22,649,337	40
Nevada	4,874,292	47
New Hampshire	15,171,504	43
New Jersey	162,741,774	15

(continued)

Toxic Pollution Released by Manufacturing Industries, 1988 (by State) (*cont'd*)

State	Total Release (pounds)	Rank
New Mexico	24,398,821	39
New York	172,106,105	14
North Carolina	136,857,071	17
North Dakota	1,394,580	52
Ohio	375,989,294	3
Oklahoma	51,720,309	31
Oregon	33,604,243	35
Pennsylvania	201,102,129	10
Puerto Rico	28,842,935	37
Rhode Island	12,568,955	45
South Carolina	82,177,534	23
South Dakota	3,059,629	48
Tennessee	249,417,227	7
Texas	724,477,706	2
Utah	137,472,389	16
Vermont	2,374,596	50
Virgin Islands	1,633,634	51
Virginia	196,619,903	11
Washington	50,338,221	32
West Virginia	57,901,379	29
Wisconsin	105,049,429	21
Wyoming	45,464,978	33
Total	6,241,030,746	

Note: The 1988 Toxic Release Inventory lists the reported release, both legal and accidental, of 302 individual toxic chemicals and 20 categories of chemical compounds regulated by the EPA. The list includes common chemicals such as ammonia, benzene, copper, vinyl chloride, and freon, as well as specialized chemicals such as hydrogen cyanide and hydrochloric acid. (For a complete list see EPA 1988b.)

The chemicals covered range in toxicity from acutely lethal to hazardous. The releases reported include emissions into air, wastewater discharge, landfill disposal, and injection well disposal.

Source: Environmental Protection Agency, 1990, *Toxins in the Community: National and Local Perspectives* (Washington, DC: GPO).

Appendix 3

Oil and Hazardous Waste Spills in and around U.S. Waters, 1970–1986

	Oil Spills	
Year	Thousands of Spills	Millions of Gallons
1970	3.71	15.25
1971	8.74	8.84
1972	9.93	18.81
1973	13.23	22.11
1974	14.43	19.42
1975	12.78	22.24
1976	13.93	36.61
1977	15.33	11.25
1978	14.50	17.56
1979	13.13	13.66
1980	11.16	15.09
1981	10.56	19.77
1982	10.41	23.15
1983	11.35	30.08
1984	13.02	18.16
1985	10.99	23.97
1986	9.21	5.53
	Hazardous Waste Spills	
Year	Number of Spills	Millions of Pounds
1970	na	na
1971	na	na
1972	na	na
1973	na	na
1974	42	1.12
1975	42	3.08
1976	54	13.16
1977	57	0.85
1978	49	0.24
1979	47	1.74

(*continued*)

Oil and Hazardous Waste Spills in and around U.S. Waters, 1970–1986
(*continued*)

	Hazardous Waste Spills	
Year	Number of Spills	Millions of Pounds
1980	63	0.27
1981	102	0.55
1982	175	8.66
1983	1,031	3.41
1984	1,433	3.80
1985	na	na
1986	na	na

na = not available

Sources: U.S. Department of Transportation, United States Coast Guard, Polluting Incidents in and around U.S. Waters, Annual, COMDTINST M16450 series, Washington, DC; Council on Environmental Quality, 1990, *Environmental Quality 1990* (Washington, DC: GPO).

Appendix 4

Public Opinion on Environmental Issues

Percentage of the U.S. Public Saying We Are Spending Too Little to Solve Environmental Problems, 1973–1988

Year	Percent
1973	45
1980	47
1983	48
1984	54
1985	56
1986	59
1987	54
1988	62

Source: Roper Reports 89-1 (January 1989), 63.
For complete discussion see Mitchell (1990:92).

Percentage of U.S. Public Prepared to Sacrifice Economic Growth to Protect Environmental Quality, 1976–1986

Year	Sacrifice Economic Growth	Sacrifice Environmental Quality
1976	38%	21%
1977	39%	26%
1978	37%	23%
1979	37%	32%
1980	—	—
1981	41%	26%
1982	41%	31%
1983	42%	16%
1984	42%	27%
1985	53%	23%
1986	58%	19%

Source: Cambridge Reports, Inc. (1986:9). For full discussion see Dunlap (1989:108–9).

Appendix 5

Membership in Selected Environmental Groups, 1980 and 1989

Group	1980	1989	Average Annual Increase
Defenders of Wildlife	44,000	80,000	9%
Environmental Defense Fund	45,000	100,000	14%
National Audibon Society	412,000	575,000	4%
Natural Resources Defense Council	42,000	117,000	20%
Sierra Club	180,000	496,000	20%
Wilderness Society	45,000	317,000	67%

Note: 1989 membership figures are from May 1989 and do not reflect the membership increase which came as a result of the Exxon Valdez oil spill.

Sources: James A. Tober, 1989, *Wildlife and the Public Interest*, (NY: Praeger); Charles Mohr, "Environmental Groups Gain in Wake of Spill," *New York Times*, June 11, 1989, 31; Robert Cameron Mitchell, 1990, "Public Opinion and the Green Lobby: Poised for the 1990s?" In *Environmental Policy in the 1990s*, ed. Norman Vig and Michael Kraft (Washington, DC: Congressional Quarterly Press).

Notes

Chapter 2

1. For a more complex discussion on the relationship between language and power see the work on discourse theory, such as Michel Foucault's *The Discourse on Language* (1971).

Chapter 7

1. For a detailed discussion of energy policy and fuel policy histories, see David Davis *Energy Politics*, 4th edition (1993).

Chapter 8

1. For a full discussion on free market environmentalism and property rights approaches see Terry Anderson and Donald Leal, *Free Market Environmentalism* (1991). In addition, John DeWitt, *Civic Environmentalism* (1994), provides an excellent discussion on how free market environmentalism may compliment the existing environmental regulatory subsystem.

2. In *Earth in the Balance*, Gore writes, "I have come to believe that we must take bold and unequivocal action: we must make the rescue of the environment the central organizing principle for civilization" (1992:269). The book is a passionate plea for re-evaluating modern assumptions. But, while pointing out the vast environmental problems, Gore fails to identify substantive policies. This, perhaps, was not his goal, nor his responsibility. Rather, the book may serve as a consciousness raising device. Still Gore does describe a "Global Marshall Plan," focusing on six elements:

(1) The stabilization of the world population, particularly in developing nations.
(2) The creation and development of environmentally appropriate technologies, which should then be made available to all nations.

(3) Change the "economic 'rules of the road' by which we measure the impact of our decisions on the environment." This would include a system of "economic accounting" assigning market value by global agreement to "ecological consequences" of individual, corporate, and national "choices in the marketplace." (1992:306)

(4) The creation of "a new generation of international agreements that will embody the . . . mechanisms . . . necessary to make the overall plan a success." (1992:306)

(5) The creation of a "cooperative plan for educating the world's citizens about our global environment" through systematic collection and dissemination of environmental data. This would "foster new patterns of thinking about the relationship of civilization to the global environment." (1992:306–7)

(6) Finally, as an integrating goal, Gore seeks "the establishment, especially in the developing world, of the social and political conditions conducive to the emergence of sustainable societies." (1992:307)

Gore accurately recognizes that it is necessary to change the way people think about civilization and the environment. Still there is a paternalism in the way he seems to be suggesting that the major problems of degradation reside in nonindustrial and less developed nations. This ignores the reality that it is the industrial nations, particularly the United States, that are the major sources of environmental degradation. In this way, Gore's passionate call for action seems to suggest that the United States has no compelling reason to substantively change the way we live—such as moving away from market allocation systems- -but we have a moral responsibility to cure the "dysfunction" in the "Third World." Such paternalism may go farther in legitimizing U.S. dysfunction than in solving global environmental degradation.

References

Abramson, Paul. 1983. *Political Attitudes in America*. San Francisco: W.H. Freeman and Co.

Abramson, Rudy. 1993. "Clinton Creates New Environmental Unit." *Los Angeles Times*. 9 February.

Ackland, Len, ed. 1972. *Credibility Gap: A Digest of the Pentagon Papers*. Philadelphia: The National Peace Literature Service.

Adler, Norman, and Charles Harrington. 1970. *The Learning of Political Behavior.* Glenview, IL: Scott, Foresman and Co.

Adorno, T. W., E. Frenkel-Brunswik, D. J. Levinson, and R. N. Sanford. 1950. *The Authoritarian Personality*. New York: Harper & Row.

Amy, Douglas J. 1990. "Environmental Dispute Resolution: The Promise and the Pitfalls." In *Environmental Policy in the 1990s.* edited by Norman Vig and Michael Kraft. Washington, DC: Congressional Quarterly Press.

Anderson, Terry L., and Donald R. Leal. 1991. *Free Market Environmentalism*. San Francisco: Pacific Research Institute for Public Policy.

Appleby, Joyce. 1984. *Capitalism and a New Social Order*. NY: New York University Press.

Associated Press. 1989. "Breakthrough Pact on Auto Smog." *San Francisco Chronicle*. 3 October. A1.

———. 1990. "PAC Money Tied to Clean Air Bills." *San Francisco Chronicle*. 23 September.

———. 1990b. "Tobacco Ties to 6 on EPA Panel." *San Francisco Chronicle*. November 9. A17.

Bachrach, Kenneth, and Alex J. Zautra. 1985. "Coping with a Community Stresser: The Threat of a Hazardous Waste Facility." *Journal of Health and Social Behavior* 26 (June):127–41.

Bartlett, Robert. 1994. "Evaluating Environmental Policy." In *Environmental Policy in the 1990s*. 2nd Edition. Edited by Norman Vig and Michael Kraft. Washington, D.C.: Congressional Quarterly Press.

Battistoni, Richard. 1985. *Public Schooling and the Education of Democratic Citizens*. Jackson, MS: University Press of Mississippi.

Beard, Charles. 1936. *An Economic Interpretation of the Constitution of the United States*. New York: MacMillan.

Bellah, Robert, Richard Madsen, William Sullivan, Ann Swidler, and Steven Tipton. 1985. *Habits of the Heart: Individualism and Commitment in American Life*. Berkeley: University of California Press.

Benson, Robert. 1993. "Making Hay on Trade, Making Hash of Our Laws." *Los Angeles Times*. November 15, B15.

Bentham, Jeremy. [1843.] 1931. "Principles of the Civil Code." In *The Theory of Legislation*. Edited by CK Ogden. London: Paul, Trench, Trubner.

Berkhofer, Robert F. 1978. *The White Man's Indian: Images of the American Indian from Columbus to the Present*. New York: Knopf.

Beswick, Carole. 1989. "In Weighing the Costs of Clean Air, Don't Omit the Value of Each Breath." *Los Angeles Times*. 8 November, pt. 2, 13.

Bowles, Samuel, and Herbert Gintis. 1986. *Democracy and Capitalism: Property, Community, and the Contradictions of Modern Social Thought*. New York: Basic Books, Inc.

Boyle, Robert H., John Graves, T. H. Watkins. 1971. *The Water Hustlers*. San Francisco: Sierra Club.

Brams, Steven J. 1985. *Rational Politics: Decisions, Games, and Strategies*. Washington, DC: Congressional Quarterly Press.

Braverman, Harry. 1974. *Labor and Monopoly Capital*. New York: Monthly Review Press.

British Petroleum. 1991. *BP Statistical Review of World Energy*. London: Corporate Communication Services Inc., June.

Brown, Lester. 1992. *State of the World 1992: A Worldwatch Report on Progress toward a Sustainable Society*. New York: W. W. Norton & Co.

———. 1993. *State of the World 1993: A Worldwatch Report on Progress toward a Sustainable Society*. New York: W. W. Norton & Co.

Brown, Lester, Christopher Flavin, and Hal Kane. 1992. *Vital Signs 1992*. New York: W. W. Norton.

Brown, Lester, Christopher Flavin, and Sandra Postel. 1991. *Saving the Planet: How to Shape an Environmentally Sustainable Global Economy*. New York: W. W. Norton & Co.

Brown, Michael. 1980. *Laying Waste: The Poisoning of America by Toxic Chemicals*. New York: Pantheon Books.

Brown, Robert. 1956. *Charles Beard and the Constitution: A Critical Analysis of "An Economic Interpretation of the Constitution."* Princeton, NJ: Princeton University Press.

Burke, Kenneth. 1966. *Language as Symbolic Action*. Berkeley: University of California Press.

Cahn, Matthew Alan, and Sheldon Kamieniecki. 1993. "Bureaucratic Politics and Environmental Policy in the Western States." In *Environmental Politics and Policy in the West*. Edited by Zachary Smith. Dubuque, IA: Kendall/Hunt Publishing Company.

California History Center. 1981. *Water in the Santa Clara Valley: A History*. Santa Clara, CA: De Anza College.

California Journal. 1991. *1991 Roster and Government Guide*. Sacramento: California Journal.

Calvert, Jerry. 1989. "Party Politics and Environmental Policy." In *Environmental Politics and Policy: Theories and Evidence*. Edited by James Lester. Durham, NC: Duke University Press.

Carmines, Edward G., and James A. Stimson. 1981. "Issue Evolution, Normal Partisan Replacement, and Normal Partisan Change." *American Political Science Review* 75:108–18.

Carr, Richard K. 1955. *American Democracy in Theory and Practice*. New York: Rinehart and Company, Inc.

Carson, Rachel. 1962. *Silent Spring*. Boston: Houghton Mifflin.

Caulfield, Henry. 1989. "The Conservation and Environmental Movements: An Historical Analysis." In *Environmental Politics and Policy: Theories and Evidence*. Edited by James Lester. Durham, NC: Duke University Press.

Christensen, Terry, and Larry Gerston. 1988. *Politics in the Golden State: The California Connection*. Boston: Scott Foresman and Co.

Clinton, Bill, and Al Gore. 1992. *Putting People First*. New York: Times Books.

Cobb, Roger, and Charles Elder. 1983a. *The Political Uses of Symbols*. New York: Longman Inc.

———. 1983b. *Participation in American Politics: The Dynamics of Agenda-Building.* 2nd Edition. Boston: Allyn and Bacon, Inc.

Cohen, Steven. 1986. "EPA: A Qualified Success." In *Controversies in Environmental Policy.* Edited by Sheldon Kamieniecki, Robert O'Brien, and Michael Clark. Albany: State University of New York Press.

Cohen, Steven, and Sheldon Kamieniecki. 1991. *Environmental Regulation through Strategic Planning.* San Francisco: Westview Press.

Cohen, William, and John Kaplan. 1982. *Constitutional Law: Civil Liberty and Individual Rights.* 2nd Edition. Mineola, NY: Foundation Press, Inc.

Coe, Richard, and Charles Wilber. 1985. *Capitalism and Democracy: Schumpeter Revisited.* Notre Dame, IN: University of Notre Dame Press.

Commoner, Barry. 1971. *The Closing Circle: Nature, Man, and Technology.* New York: Knopf.

Comp, T. Allen, ed. 1989. *Blueprint for the Environment : A Plan for Federal Action.* Salt Lake City: Howe Brothers.

Conservation Foundation. 1984. *State of the Environment: An Assessment at Mid-Decade.* Washington, D.C.: Conservation Foundation.

———. 1987. *State of the Environment: A View toward the Nineties.* Washington, DC: Conservation Foundation.

Converse, Philip E. 1964. "The Nature of Belief Systems in Mass Publics." In *Ideology and Discontent.* Edited by David Apter. New York: Free Press.

Corson, Walter H., ed. 1990. *The Global Ecology Handbook.* Boston: Beacon Press.

Council on Environmental Quality (CEQ). 1979. *Environmental Quality 1979.* Washington, DC: GPO.

———. 1980. *Environmental Quality 1980.* Washington, D.C.: GPO.

———. 1990. *Environmental Quality Twentieth Annual Report.* Washington, DC: GPO.

———. 1992. *Environmental Quality Twenty-Second Annual Report.* Washington, DC: GPO.

Dahl, Robert. 1985. *A Preface to Economic Democracy.* Berkeley: University of California Press.

Daly, Herman E. 1991. *Steady-State Economics.* 2nd Edition. Washington, DC: Island Press.

Davis, Charles, and James Lester. 1989. "Federalism and Environmental Policy." In *Environmental Politics and Policy: Theories and Evidence.* Edited by James Lester. Durham, NC: Duke University Press.

Davis, David. 1993. *Energy Politics.* 4th Edition. New York: St. Martin's Press.

Dawson, Richard, Kenneth Prewitt, and Karen Dawson. 1977. *Political Socialization.* 2nd Edition. Boston: Little, Brown and Co.

Debo, Angie. 1970. *A History of the Indians of the United States.* Norman: University of Oklahoma Press.

DeFleur, Melvin. 1970. *Theories of Mass Communication.* 2nd Edition. NY: David McKay Co., Inc.

Dennis, Jack, ed. 1973. *Socialization to Politics.* NY: John Wiley & Sons, Inc.

Department of Commerce. 1989. *Statistical Abstract of the United States, 1989.* Washington, DC: GPO.

Diamond, Edwin, and Stephen Bates. 1986. *The Spot: The Rise of Political Advertising on Television.* Cambridge: MIT Press.

Dickinson, H. T. 1977. *Liberty and Property: Political Ideology in Eighteenth Century Britain.* New York: Holmes and Meier.

Dinan, Terry, and F. Reed Johnson. 1990. "Effects of Hazardous Waste Risks on Property Transfers: Legal Liability vs. Direct Regulation." *Natural Resources Journal* 30 (Summer).

Domhoff, G. William. 1983. *Who Rules America Now?* New York: Simon and Schuster, Inc.

Dowie, Mark. 1977. "Pinto Madness." *Mother Jones.* Vol. 2, No. 8, September/October.

Downs, Anthony. 1957. *An Economic Theory of Democracy.* New York: Harper and Row.

———. 1972. "Up and Down with Ecology: The 'Issue- Attention Cycle.'" *Public Interest* 28:38–50.

Duerksen, Christopher. 1983. *Environmental Regulation of Industrial Plant Siting.* Washington, DC: The Conservation Foundation.

Dunlap, Riley E. 1989. "Public Interest and Environmental Policy." In *Environmental Politics and Policy.* Edited by James Lester. Durham: Duke University Press.

Dye, Thomas R. 1986. *Who's Running America? The Conservative Years.* 4th Edition. Englewood Cliffs, NJ: Prentice-Hall, Inc.

Earth Works Group. 1990. *The Recycler's Handbook.* Berkeley: Earth Works Press.

Easton, David. 1965. *A Systems Analysis of Political Life.* NY: John Wiley & Sons, Inc.

Easton, David, and Jack Dennis. 1969. *Children in the Political System.* NY: McGraw-Hill Book Co.

Edelman, Murray. 1971. *Politics as Symbolic Action.* Chicago: Markham Publishing Company.

———. 1973. "The State as a Provider of Symbolic Outputs." Presented at the World Congress of the International Political Science Association, Montreal, August 1973.

———. 1977. *Political Language: Words That Succeed and Policies That Fail.* NY: Academic Press of Harcourt Brace Jovanovich.

———. 1988. *Constructing the Political Spectacle.* Chicago: The University of Chicago Press.

Energy Information Administration (EIA). 1992. *International Energy Annual 1990.* Washington, DC: Department of Energy.

Environmental Protection Agency (EPA). 1988a. *Report to Congress: Solid Waste Disposal in the United States.* Volume II. Washington, DC: GPO. October.

———. 1988b. *The Waste System.* Washington, DC: GPO. November.

———. 1989a. *National Air Pollution Emission Estimates. 1940–87.* Research Triangle Park, NC: EPA.

———. 1989b. *Superfund National Priority List.* Washington, DC: GPO.

———. 1990a, "National Air Quality and Emissions Trends Report, 1988." Research Triangle Park, NC: EPA.

———. 1990b. *Toxics in the Community: National and Local Perspectives.* Washington, DC: GPO.

Epstein, Edward Jay. 1974. *News from Nowhere: Television and the News.* New York: Random House.

Evans, Sara, and Harry Boyte. 1986. *Free Spaces: The Sources of Democratic Change in America.* New York: Harper and Row.

Foucault, Michel. 1971. *The Discourse on Language.* Translated by Rupert Swyer. Published as an appendix to the American edition of *The Archeology of Knowledge. L'ordre du discours: Lecon inaugurale au College de France prononcee le 2 decembre 1970.* Pairs: Gallimard.

Frederickson, George M. 1981. *White Supremacy.* New York: Oxford University Press.

Freeman, A. Myrick, 1990. "Water Pollution Policy." *Public Policies for Environmental Protection*. Edited by Paul Portney. Washington, DC: Resources for the Future.

Friedman, Milton. 1982. *Capitalism and Freedom*. Chicago: The University of Chicago Press.

Garramone, Gina, and Charles Atkin. 1986. "Mass Communication and Political Socialization: Specifying the Effects." *Public Opinion Quarterly*. 50:76–86.

General Accounting Office (GAO). 1986a. "The Nation's Water: Key Unanswered Questions about the Quality of Rivers and Streams." Report No. GAO/PEMD-86-6 (September).

———. 1986b. "Chemical Data: EPA's Data Collection Practices and Procedures on Chemicals," Report No. GAO/RCED 88-127 (April).

———. 1987. "Extent of Nation's Potential Hazardous Waste Problem Still Unknown." Report Number GAO/RCED-88–44. (December).

Goldfarb, William. 1988. *Water Law*. 2nd Edition. Chelsea, MI: Lewis Publishers.

Goldstein, Robert. 1978. *Political Repression in Modern America*. Cambridge: Schenkman Publishing Co.

Gore, Al. 1992. *Earth in the Balance: Ecology and the Human Spirit*. New York: Plume.

Gottlieb, Robert. 1988. *A Life of Its Own : The Politics and Power of Water*. New York: Harcourt Brace Jovanovich.

Graebner, William. 1987. *The Engineering of Consent: Democracy and Authority in Twentieth-Century America*. Madison: The University of Wisconsin Press.

Gramsci, Antonio. [1935.] 1971. "The Intellectuals." In *Selections from the Prison Notebooks*. Edited by Quintin Hoare and Geoffrey Nowell Smith. New York: International Publishers.

Greenberg, Edward, ed. 1970. *Political Socialization*. New York: Atherton Press.

———. 1986. *The American Political System: A Radical Approach*. 4th Edition. Boston: Little, Brown and Co.

Grey, Thomas. 1983. *The Legal Enforcement of Reality*. New York: Alfred A. Knopf.

Gruber, Michael. 1988. "Are Today's Institutional Tools Up to the Task?" *EPA Journal* 14(7):2–6.

Guttman, Daniel, and Barry Willner. 1976. *The Shadow Government*. New York: Pantheon Books.

Hamilton, Alexander, James Madison, John Jay. 1961. *The Federalist Papers.* Edited by Clinton Rossiter. New York: New American Library.

Hardin, Garrett. 1968. "The Tragedy of the Commons." *Science,* 162 (December):1243–48.

Hartz, Louis. 1955. *The Liberal Tradition in America.* New York: Harcourt Brace Jovanovich.

Heilbroner, Robert L. 1977. *The Economic Transformation of America.* New York: Harcourt Brace Jovanovich.

———. 1980. *An Inquiry into the Human Prospect.* New York: W. W. Norton, Company.

Herman, Edward, and Noam Chomsky. 1988. *Manufacturing Consent: The Political Economy of the Mass Media.* New York: Pantheon Books.

High Country News, eds. 1987. *Western Water Made Simple.* Washington, DC: Island Press.

Hines, Lawrence Gregory. 1988. *The Market, Energy, and the Environment.* Boston: Allyn and Bacon, Inc.

Hofstadter, Richard. 1948. *The American Political Tradition.* New York: Knopf.

Holdren, John P. 1991. "Energy in Transition," In *Energy for Planet Earth.* Edited by Scientific America. New York: W. H. Freeman and Co.

Hume, David. 1948. "Of the Original Contract." In *Hume's Moral and Political Philosophy.* Edited by Henry Aiken. New York: Hafner Press.

Hyman, Herbert. 1959. *Political Socialization: A Study in the Psychology of Political Behavior.* New York: The Free Press.

Iyengar, Shanto and Donald R. Kinder. 1987. *News That Matters: Television and American Opinion.* Chicago: The University of Chicago Press.

Jacob, Herbert. 1984. *Justice in America: Courts, Lawyers, and the Judicial Process.* 4th Edition. Boston: Little, Brown and Co.

Jones, Charles. 1974. "Speculative-Augmentation in Federal Air Pollution Policy Making." *Journal of Politics.* 36:453.

Kairys, David, ed. 1982. *The Politics of Law: A Progressive Critique.* New York: Pantheon Books.

Kamieniecki, Sheldon, Matthew Alan Cahn, and Eugene Goss. 1991. "Western Governments and Environmental Policy." In *Politics and Public Policy in the Contemporary American West.* Edited by Clive Thomas. Albuquerque: University of New Mexico Press.

Kamieniecki, Sheldon, and Michael R. Ferrall. 1991. "Intergovernmental Relations and Clean-Air Policy in Southern California." *Publius: The Journal of Federalism* 21(Summer).

Kann, Mark E. 1986. "Environmental Democracy in the United States." In *Controversies in Environmental Policy*. Edited by Sheldon Kamieniecki, Robert O'Brien, and Michael Clarke. Albany: State University of New York Press.

———. 1991. *On the Man Question: Gender and Civic Virtue in America*. Philadelphia: Temple University Press.

Kelly, Alfred, Winfred Harbison and Herman Belz. 1983. *The American Constitution: Its Origins and Development*. New York: W. W. Norton, Co.

Kenski, Henry, and Helen Ingram. 1986. "The Reagan Administration and Environmental Regulation: The Constraint of the Political Market." In *Controversies in Environmental Policy*. Edited by Sheldon Kamieniecki, Robert O'Brien, and Michael Clarke. New York: State University of New York Press.

Kenworthy, Tom. 1992. "Drawing a Line on the Environment." *The Washington Post National Weekly Edition*. December 21–27:15.

———. 1993. "Babbitt: A Conservationist Takes Over at Interior." *The Washington Post National Weekly Edition*. January 4–10:14.

Key, V. O. 1961. *Public Opinion and American Democracy*. New York: Knopf.

Kinder, Donald, and David Sears. 1985. "Public Opinion and Political Action." In *Handbook of Social Psychology*. 3rd Edition. Edited by G. Lindzey and E. Aronson. Reading, MA: Addison-Wesley. Vol. 2:659–741.

Kraft, Michael E. 1993. "Air Pollution in the West: Testing the Limits of Public Support with Southern California's Clean Air Policy." In *Environmental Politics and Policy in the West*. Edited by Zachary A. Smith. Dubuque, IA: Kendall/Hunt Publishing Company.

Kraft, Michael E., and Bruce B. Clary. 1991, "Citizen Participation and the NIMBY Syndrome: Public Response to Radioactive Waste Disposal." *The Western Political Quarterly*. 44(June):2.

Kutler, Stanley, ed. 1984. *The Supreme Court and the Constitution: Readings in American Constitutional History*. 3rd Edition. New York: W. W. Norton & Co.

Lane, Robert. 1962. *Political Ideology: Why the American Common Man Believes What He Does*. New York: The Free Press of Glencoe.

Lasswell, Harold. 1938. *Politics: Who Gets What, When, and How*. New York: McGraw-Hill.

Lave, Lester B. 1981. "An Economist's View." In *The Scientific Basis of Health and Safety Regulations*. Edited by Robert Crandell and Lester Lave. Washington, DC: Brookings.

Leatherman, Stephen. 1988. "Likely Sea Level Rise." Paper presented at the second North American Conference on Preparing for Climate Change. Washington, DC, December 6.

Lester, James, ed. 1989. *Environmental Politics and Policy: Theories and Evidence*. Durham, NC: Duke University Press.

———. 1989. "A New Federalism? Environmental Policy in the States." In Lester.

Lindblom, Charles. 1959. "The Science of Muddling Through." *Public Administration Review*. 19(Spring):79–88.

Lippman, Thomas W. 1991. "Conservationists, Start Your Engines." *The Washington Post National Weekly Edition*. February 18–24:35.

———. 1993. "For the Energy Nominee, an Arms Gap." *The Washington Post National Weekly Edition*. December 28-January 3:15.

Lippmann, Walter. 1922. *Public Opinion*. New York: The Free Press.

Liroff, Richard A. 1986. *Reforming Air Pollution Regulation: The Toil and Trouble of EPA's Bubble*. Washington DC: The Conservation Foundation.

Lloyd, W. F. 1833. *Two Lectures on the Checks to Population*. Oxford: Oxford University Press. Reprinted in part in Garrett Hardin. 1964. *Population, Evolution, and Birth Control*. San Francisco: Freeman.

Locke, John. 1963. *Two Treatises of Government*. Edited by Peter Laslett. New York: New American Library.

Los Angeles Times. 1990. "EPA Panel Calls Second Hand Smoke a Carcinogen." *San Francisco Chronicle*. December 6, A18.

Lowery, Shearon, and Melvin DeFleur. 1983. *Milestones in Mass Communication Research: Media Effects*. New York: Longman.

Lowi, Theodore, and Benjamin Ginsberg. 1990. *American Government: Freedom and Power*. New York: W. W. Norton Co.

Lutz, William. 1989. *Doublespeak*. New York: Harper Perennial.

Machiavelli, Niccolo. 1983. *The Prince, The Discourses*. In *The Portable Machiavelli*. Edited by Peter Bondanella and Mark Muse. New York: Penguin Books.

Macpherson, C. B. 1977. *The Life and Times of Liberal Democracy*. New York: Oxford University Press.

———. 1962. *The Political Theory of Possessive Individualism: Hobbes to Locke*. London: Oxford University Press.

Mandel, Bill. 1991. "Gloating Lasts Longer than Gulf War." *San Francisco Examiner*. May 19, B2.

Mansbridge, Jane J. 1990. "The Rise and Fall of Self-Interest in the Explanation of Political Life." In *Beyond Self Interest*. Edited by Jane J. Mansbridge. Chicago: The University of Chicago Press.

Marchetti, Victor, and John Marks. 1980. *The CIA and the Cult of Intelligence*. New York: Del Publishing Co., Inc.

Marcus, Alfred A. 1986. "EPA's Successes and Failures." In *Controversies in Environmental Policy*. Edited by Sheldon Kamieniecki, Robert O'Brien, and Michael Clarke. New York: State University of New York Press.

Markovich, Denise, and Ronald Pynn. 1988. *American Political Economy: Using Economics with Politics*. Belmont, CA: Wadsworth.

Marvick, Dwaine, ed. 1977. *Harold D. Lasswell on Political Sociology*. Chicago: The University of Chicago Press.

Mason, Alpheas, and D. Grier Stephenson, Jr. 1987. *American Constitutional Law*. Englewood Cliffs, NJ: Princeton-Hall, Inc.

Mathews, Jay. 1989. "Solar Energy Complex Hailed as Beacon for Utility Innovation." *The Washington Post*. March 2, A25.

McCurdy, Howard. 1986. "Environmental Protection and the New Federalism: The Sagebrush Rebellion and Beyond." In *Controversies in Environmental Policy*. Edited by Sheldon Kamieniecki, Robert O'Brien, and Michael Clarke. New York: State University of New York Press.

McDonald, Forrest. 1958. *We the People: The Economic Origins of the Constitution*. Chicago: The University of Chicago Press.

McWilliams, Wilson Cary. 1973. *The Idea of Fraternity in America*. Berkeley: University of California Press.

Meier, Kenneth J. 1985. *Regulation: Politics, Bureaucracy and Economics*. New York: St. Martin's Press.

Milbrath, Lester W. 1989. *Envisioning a Sustainable Society: Learning Our Way Out*. Albany: State University of New York Press.

Mill, James. 1820. "An Essay on Government." Barker edition. Cambridge: The University Press, 1937.

Mills, C. W. 1956. *The Power Elite*. Oxford: Oxford University Press.

Mitchell, Robert Cameron. 1990. "Public Opinion and the Green Lobby: Poised for the 1990s?" In *Environmental Policy in the 1990s*. Edited by Norman Vig and Michael Kraft. Washington, D.C.: Congressional Quarterly Press.

Mosher, Lawrence. 1980. "Environmentalists Question Whether to Retreat or Stay on the Offensive." *National Journal.* 13(December):2116.

Moskowitz, Milton, Michael Katz, and Robert Levering, eds. 1982. *Everybody's Business: An Almanac.* New York: Harper and Row.

National Research Council. 1987. *Geothermal Energy Technology: Issues, Research, and Development Needs, and Cooperative Arrangements.* Washington, DC: National Academy Press.

Navarro, Peter. 1984. *The Policy Game: How Special Interests and Ideologues are Stealing America.* Lexington: Lexington Books.

———. 1980. "The Politics of Air Pollution." *The Public Interest.* (Spring):36–44.

Neustadt, Richard. 1980. *Presidential Power.* New York: John Wiley and Sons, Inc.

New York Times. 1988a. 28 July.

———. 1988b. 13 December.

———. 1988c. 27 October

———. 1989a. 13 November.

———. 1989b. 14 December.

Nimmo, Dan, and Keith Sanders, eds. 1981. *Handbook of Political Communication.* Beverly Hills: Sage Publications.

Nozick, Robert. 1974. *Anarchy, State, and Utopia.* New York: Basic Books.

Nuclear Regulatory Commission (NRC). 1993. Public Affairs Office, telephone interview, November 18.

Nunn, Clyde Z., Harry J. Crockett, Jr., and J. Allen Williams, Jr. 1978. *Tolerance for Nonconformity: A National Survey of Americans' Changing Commitment to Civil Liberties.* San Francisco: Jossey-Bass.

O'Brien, Rory. 1992. *The Normative and the Empirical: Justice and Water Distribution in Three Western States.* Dissertation, Los Angeles, University of Southern California.

Oil and Gas Journal. 1990. Vol. 88, No. 53. Tulsa: Pennwell Publishing Co., December.

O'Leary, Philip, et al. 1988. "Managing Solid Waste." *Scientific American.* December.

Omenn, Gilbert, and Lester Lave. 1981. *Clearing the Air: Reforming the Clean Air Act.* Washington DC: The Brookings Institute.

Ophuls, William. 1977. *Ecology and the Politics of Scarcity*. San Francisco: W. H. Freeman and Company.

Orr, David W. 1992. *Ecological Literacy*. Albany: State University of New York Press.

Orren, Gary, and Nelson Polsby, eds. 1987. *Media and Momentum: The New Hampshire Primary*. Chatham, NJ: Chatham House Publishers, Inc.

Paehlke, Robert C. 1989. *Environmentalism and the Future of Progressive Politics*. New Haven, CT: Yale University Press.

Page, Benjamin, and Robert Shapiro. 1992. *The Rational Public: Fifty Years of Trends in Americans' Policy Preferences*. Chicago: University of Chicago Press.

Parenti, Michael. 1988. *Democracy for the Few*. 5th Edition. New York: St. Martin's Press.

Peters, B. Guy. 1993. *American Public Policy: Promise and Performance*. 3rd Edition. Chatham, NJ: Chatham House Publishers.

Piasecki, Bruce. 1993. "The Green Machine Is Asleep at the Switch." *Los Angeles Times*. November 1, B13.

Piven, Frances Fox, and Richard A. Cloward. 1982. *The New Class War*. New York: Pantheon Books.

Pocock, J. G. A. 1975. *The Machiavellian Moment: Florintine Political Thought and the Republican Tradition*. Princeton: Princeton University Press.

Pollock, Cynthia. 1987. *Mining Urban Wastes: The Potential for Recycling*. Worldwatch Paper 76. Washington, DC: Worldwatch Institute. April.

Portney, Paul R. 1990. "EPA and the Evolution of Federal Regulation." *Public Policies for Environmental Protection*. Edited by Paul Portney. Washington, DC: Resources for the Future.

Postel, Sandra. 1993. "Facing Water Scarcity." In *State of the World 1993*. Edited by Lester Brown. New York: W. W. Norton & Co.

Presthus, Robert. 1974. *Elites in the Policy Process*. Cambridge: Cambridge University Press.

Price, Sylvia A., and Lorraine M. Wilson. 1986. *Pathophysiology: Clinical Concepts of Disease Processes*. 3rd Edition. New York: McGraw-Hill Book Company.

Pytte, Alyson. 1990a. "A Decade's Acrimony Lifted in the Glow of Clean Air." *Congressional Quarterly Weekly Report*. October 27, 3587–92.

———. 1990b. "Provisions: Clean Air Act Amendments." *Congressional Quarterly Weekly Report*. November 24, 3934–63.

Rabinovitch, John David. 1981. "The Politics of Poison." In *Who's Poisoning America*. Edited by Ralph Nadar, Ronald Brownstein, and John Richard. San Francisco: Sierra Club Books.

Rawls, John. 1971. *A Theory of Justice*. Cambridge, MA: The Belknap Press of Harvard University Press.

Regens, James L., and Robert W. Rycroft. 1988. *The Acid Rain Controversy*. Pittsburgh: The University of Pittsburgh Press.

Renshon, Stanley Allen, ed. 1977. *Handbook of Political Socialization*. New York: The Free Press.

Reynolds, H. T., and David Vogler. 1991. *Governing America*. New York: Harper-Collins Publishers.

Risen, James. 1993. "Clinton Kills Controversial Quayle Panel." *Los Angeles Times*. January 23, A14.

Rogin, Michael. 1987. *Ronald Reagan the Movie, and Other Episodes in Political Demonology*. Berkeley: University of California Press.

Rosenbaum, Walter. 1985. *Environmental Politics and Policy*. Washington DC: CQ Press.

———. 1989. "The Bureaucracy and Environmental Policy." In *Environmental Politics and Policy: Theories and Evidence*. Edited by James Lester. Durham, NC: Duke University Press.

———. 1991. *Environmental Politics and Policy*. 2nd. Edition. Washington, DC: CQ Press.

Rosenberg, Shawn. 1987. "Reason and Ideology: Interpreting People's Understanding of American Politics." *Polity* 20(Fall):1.

Rossiter, Clinton. 1963. *Constitutional Dictatorship*. New York: Harcourt, Brace and World, Inc.

Rourke, Francis. 1984. *Bureaucracy, Politics, and Public Policy*. 3rd Edition. Boston: Little, Brown and Company.

Royce, Knut, 1991. "Did the U.S. Distort Facts on Key Gulf Issues?" *New York Newsday*. In the *San Francisco Chronicle*, January 30, 1991. Briefing 1.

Schmandt, Jurgen. 1984. "Regulation and Science." *Science, Technology, and Human Values* 9, no. 1:23–38.

Schneider, Keith. 1992. "California Gets Pro-Environment Water Law." *New York Times*. November 1.

Schumpeter, Joseph. 1942. *Capitalism, Socialism, and Democracy.* New York: Harper and Row.

Schwartz, David, and Sandra Schwartz, eds. 1975. *New Directions in Political Socialization.* New York: The Free Press.

Scientific American. 1991. *Energy for Planet Earth.* New York: Freeman.

Shabecoff, Philip. 1990. "Bush, Senators Water Down Clean Air Bill." *New York Times.* March 2.

Simon, Julian. 1986, "Wealth in Numbers." *Development Forum* 14 (July-August).

Slovic, Paul. 1987. "Perception of Risk." *Science* 236 (April 17):280–85.

Smith, Adam. 1937 (1776). *The Wealth of Nations.* New York: Modern Library.

Smith, Zachary. 1992. *The Environmental Policy Paradox.* Englewood Cliffs, NJ: Prentice Hall.

Snell, Bradford Curie. 1985. "American Ground Transport." In *Crisis in American Institutions.* Edited by Jerome H. Skolnick and Elliott Curie. Boston: Little, Brown and Company.

Southern California Air Quality Management District (SCAQMD). 1989. Air Quality Management Plan.

Stacey, Barrie. 1977. *Political Socialization in Western Society: An Analysis from a Life-Span Perspective.* New York: St. Martin's Press.

Stouffer, Samuel A. 1955. *Communism, Conformity, and Civil Liberties: A Cross-Section of the Nation Speaks Its Mind.* Garden City, NY: Doubleday.

Tapper, Ted. 1976. *Political Education and Stability: Elite Responses to Political Conflict.* New York: John Wiley & Sons.

United States, President's Special Review Board. 1987. *The Tower Commission Report: The Full Text of the President's Special Review Board.* John Tower, Chair. New York: Bantam Books.

Vershner, Vlae. 1991. "State Turns Off Its Water Supply to Agriculture." *San Francisco Chronicle*, February 5, A1.

Vig, Norman. 1990. "Presidential Leadership: From the Reagan to the Bush Years." In *Environmental Policy in the 1990s.* Edited by Norman Vig and Michael Kraft. Washington, DC: CQ.

Vig, Norman, and Michael Kraft, eds. 1990a. *Environmental Policy in the 1990s.* Washington DC: CQ Press.

————. 1990b. "Environmental Policy from the Seventies to the Nineties: Continuity and Change." In *Environmental Policy in the 1990s*. By Norman Vig and Michael Kraft. Washington DC: CQ Press.

————. 1990c. "Presidential Styles and Substance: Environmental Policy from Reagan to Bush." A paper presented at the 1990 Annual Meeting of the American Political Science Association, San Francisco, August 30 to September 2, 1990.

————. 1994. *Environmental Policy in the 1990s*. 2nd Edition. Washington DC: CQ Press.

Viviano, Frank. 1991. "U.S. Toxics Cleanup Mired in Lawsuits." *San Francisco Chronicle*. May 29, A1.

Wald, Matthew L. 1989. "Nation Looks to California for Guidance on Pollution Laws." *San Francisco Chronicle*. A11.

————. 1990. "Where All That Gas Goes: Drivers' Thirst for Power." *The New York Times*. November 21, A1.

Walzer, Michael. 1983. *Spheres of Justice: A Defense of Pluralism and Equality*. NY: Basic Books, Inc.

Washington Post. 1988a. March 16, A1.

————. 1988b. February 24, 1988. A10.

————. 1989a. April 6, A3.

————. 1989b. July 27, A3.

————. 1990. "EPA Withdraws Tough Proposal on Recycling." *San Francisco Chronicle*, December 20, A17.

————. 1991. "U.S. Says Most Bombs Used in Gulf Missed Their Targets." In the *San Francisco Chronicle*. 16 March.

Weber, Max. [1922] 1946. "Bureaucracy." In *From Max Weber: Essays in Sociology*. Edited by H. H. Gerth and C. Wright Mills. New York: Oxford University Press.

Weber, Susan, ed. 1988. *USA by Numbers*. Washington, DC: Zero Population Growth.

Webster, Noah. [1785.] 1937. *Sketches of American Policy*. Edited by Harry R. Warfel. New York: Scholar's Facsimiles and Reprints.

Weinberg, Carl J., and Robert H. Williams. 1991. "Energy from the Sun." In *Energy for Planet Earth*. Edited by Scientific America. New York: W. H. Freeman and Co.

Weisskopf, Michael. 1986. "Did Water Kill Children in Woburn?" *The Washington Post*. April 3, A3.

Wenz, Peter S. 1988. *Environmental Justice*. Albany: State University of New York Press.

Wilkerson, Isabel. 1991. "Blacks Wary of Their Big Role in the Military." *New York Times*. December 25, A1.

Wood, Gordon. 1969. *The Creation of the American Republic, 1776–1787*. New York: W. W. Norton & Company.

World Energy Council. 1989. *1989 Survey of Energy Resources*. Federal Republic of Germany, Federal Institute for Geosciences and Natural Resources. London: World Energy Conference.*World Oil*. 1991. Vol. 212n No. 8. Houston: Gulf Publishing Co., August.

World Resources Institute. 1993. *The 1993 Information Please Environmental Almanac*. New York: Houghton Mifflin Co.

World Resources Institute (WRI) and International Institute for Environment and Development (IIED). 1987. *World Resources 1987*. New York: Basic Books, Inc.

———. 1989. *World Resources 1988–1989*. New York: Basic Books, Inc.

Wright, James D. 1976. *The Dissent of the Governed: Alienation and Democracy in America*. New York: Academic Press of Harcourt Brace Jovanovich.

Zinn, Howard. 1980. *A People's History of the United States*. New York: Harper Colophon Books.

Index